What If It DOES Work Out?

Turn your passion into cash, make an impact and live the life you were born to

By Susie Moore

Printed in the United States of America

First Printing, 2016

ISBN-13: 978-1533375032
ISBN-10: 1533375038

www.susie-moore.com

Introduction

"Remember, becoming an entrepreneur early in life is one of the hallmarks of the most successful individuals throughout modern history."
~Jack Canfield

"How dare you settle for less when the world has made it so easy for you to be remarkable?"
~Seth Godin

"What is your passion? What stirs your soul and makes you feel like you're totally in harmony with why you showed up here in the first place? Know this for certain: Whatever it may be, you can make a living doing it and simultaneously provide a service for others. I guarantee it."
~Dr. Wayne W. Dyer

What is a Side Hustle?

A side hustle is a business that generates real cash that you run on your free time. It allows you the flexibility to pursue what you're most interested in. It's a chance to delve into food, travel, fashion or **whatever you're passionate about** while maintaining your day job. It is the magical door that opens you up to major opportunities and freedom in a short period of time. It's the practical option to a corporate exit, the way to fulfill a lifelong dream and make the impact you came onto this planet to have.

This book will take you through the journey of starting a side hustle and give you the confidence and the tools you need to get your side hustle going. Know this: you are already a pro. Look at how you turn up to work or school, or conduct yourself as a parent EVERY DAY, no matter what. What you need to launch a successful side hustle is already within you. Plus, there are more options now than ever before, making entrepreneurship available to you (and they keep getting better).

The majority of millionaires have multiple revenue streams; there is no safety (or fun!) in a single paycheck. This book is your ticket to more wealth, more freedom, more security, more influence and more joy.

Chapter One: Why Are You Reading This Book?

"You don't have a career, you have a life."
~Cheryl Strayed

"Happiness is the joy that you feel when you are moving towards your potential."
~Shawn Achor

"IS this all there is?" I contemplated one morning while feeling restless at work. I was a sales director in New York for a Silicon Valley startup recently acquired by a Fortune 500 company. I was on a conference call in my freezing office, doused in artificial light, scouring Pinterest. I gazed through the window at the beautiful blue sky outside. Sigh. Then I saw a pin that struck me: a quote from poet Mary Oliver, from "The Summer Day."

> *"Tell me, what is it that you plan to do with your one wild and precious life?"*

My soul screamed: "Not only this!"
It was time for change. And so it began. My side hustle.

I've read more than 550 personal development books and I am a natural adviser to the people in my life, especially when it comes to connecting them to their purpose, becoming more confident, negotiating and networking. My side hustle, naturally, became life coaching.

After more than a decade in sales (which in large part, I loved) I felt ready for something new. I also know that as human beings we are wired for new challenges and experiences. And I'm not alone: a 2012 Gallup survey showed that only 13 percent of employees worldwide are engaged at work.

I joined New York University's coaching program and used my sales skills to pitch article ideas to editors. I wanted to get my work published so I could attract clients (it's called a hustle for a reason)!

My advice-based articles helped generate a string of clients and within a couple of months I was earning money both writing and coaching. I couldn't believe my luck! Getting paid to talk to people and give life advice? There is a God! While writing for Marie Claire I even got to interview some pretty incredible people including Arianna Huffington, Kris Jenner, and Spanx founder Sara Blakely.

Writing earned me between $75-$750 per article (from the publications that paid) and I wrote multiple pieces a month. I was typing away everywhere: on the subway, in the Whole Foods line, while on a lunch break at the office. Each piece took 2-3 hours to complete. Writing for major publications with tens of millions of monthly unique visitors not only gave me credibility, it drove traffic to my blog – resulting in additional email subscribers who in turn often sought coaching or advice from me.

I started coaching people at $100 a session and as demand increased (largely due to my content being shared) and as my life coaching skills developed, I was able to raise my prices. Working around the commitments of my day job, which included travel and after-hours client entertainment, some months I made an extra $4,000 on my side hustle. That was working 12-16 hours a week on top of my day job. According to Nielsen, the average 35-49 year old American watches more than 33 hours of television a week. You do the math.

I could not recommend side hustling more highly. You make extra money, use talents that lie dormant in your 9-5 day job – plus you're hedging your bets against an uncertain economy. Starting a business while employed also allows you to determine proof of concept more safely. This means, you prove that your product or service is wanted in the world before you dedicate your full-time focus towards it.

But it's not always a breeze. You will need a combination of creative thinking and hard work hard to attract your first clients and build your brand then manage cash flow, various administrative tasks (including outsourcing), *and* look for ways to make these more efficient, so your hustle can scale.

You have to be committed. You will have to forgo that "Game of Thrones" binge session you planned and you will often be first to leave the bar. You will have to overcome self-doubt about charging for work that a lot of the time feels like fun. "No" will be your new favorite word. BUT the pay-off can be incredible. After almost 18 months of juggling my rapidly expanding hustle, I resigned from my full-time job. This was no mean feat as my job, in that final year, grossed around $500,000. That is how much I loved and trusted in my hustle's expansion. And I grew up in a household with no money – we were on welfare in fact – so I respect money and do not take financial risk lightly.

At the end of each chapter you'll find a call to action that I've included to help you apply the principles I discuss. Homework, if you like. I hope these will keep you motivated as you read this book. I have also interspersed some interviews with badass entrepreneurs and people who've started very successful side hustles. I hope you enjoy them and learn something from them too.

I'm a lot like you; I just want freedom in my life and ownership of my work. And to make a meaningful impact in the world doing work that I love. On my terms.

To hustlers everywhere – you're not alone. This is for you.

Chapter Two:
Understanding Fear – What Is Stopping Me From Doing What I Really, Really, Really Want To Do?

"Fear kills more dreams than failure ever could."
~ Suzy Kassem, writer, poet, philosopher

"Our doubts are traitors, and make us lose the good we oft might win, by fearing to attempt."
~ William Shakespeare, "Measure for Measure"

THE worst night of my life started with some cheap Pad Thai and a bottle of Sauvignon Blanc. It was an ordinary Friday night in. Ordinary, apart from the obscene amount of tension in the air. The arguments with my then-husband had swelled to a point where the only exit was divorce – or what felt like a slow, certain death. It was an old argument too, rehashed – one I cannot even remember the details of now, but that at the time stabbed me in the heart with the realization there was no hope left. The end had arrived. I knew it then.

I heard the front door slam in anger for the last time. Bang! This time, the sound was final. "This is it," my soul heard. No turning back. I cried on the bathroom floor that night, acknowledging the truth. I had to leave.

I was in my early twenties living in Australia with little money and no family to turn to (they were back in the U.K. where I grew up). But I found an inner strength that stirred in times like these. Our internal guidance never fails us when we allow it to rise. It told me what I needed to do. I needed to make a bold move – get up, get out and start over. Immediately.

I wish I could revisit that sad, scared girl that evening and tell her that everything turns out OK. Much better than OK, even.

Was the fear of being 23, alone in a new country with little cash – and now a divorcee! – just in my mind? Hell no! I was terrified. The fear was real. Fear is always real. Fear of change is one of the biggest preventers for us changing anything in our lives at all.

I'm not here to diminish fear. I feel like I could write 300 books on the subject. It makes an appearance in almost every single blog post I have ever written. Fear manifests itself in a million ugly ways. It shows up as excuses. Or procrastination. It shows up as practicality: "Oh, I'd love to be a photographer but I can't make money that way." It shows up as confusion or ignorance: "I have no idea what my purpose is."

As a life coach the trickiest part of getting to the core of what someone wants is having them say out loud what they really, really, want. Not to me, **but to themselves**. Once we say it aloud it has a certain power. Many dreams are buried because we are too scared to voice them to ourselves. When we speak them, dreams become real. And that's terrifying because we know what we need to do.

Here is the skinny on fear:

According to Dan Baker, Ph.D., and Cameron Stauth, author of, "What Happy People Know," unless your fear is the protective force that stops you from doing something dangerous (like hitching a ride with a total stranger, for example) all fears belong to two groups. Yes, just two groups! All fears can be attributed to a belief in the following:

1. **I am not enough**
2. **I do not have enough**

As humans we have not evolved. Back in the day of the caveman these fears were real and the result of them being actualized was certain death. If you were not fit, healthy and strong, the tribe would leave you behind in order to survive. And if you did not have enough – meaning if you did not collect food every day and have the materials to give you shelter and warmth – you would perish.

And today?

Being enough in today's world means being educated, connected, charming, smart, good looking, thin, interesting... the list is endless – especially when you are busy comparing yourself to your peers.

Having enough means possessing the luxuries that we enjoy but that can also trap us – large home, fancy car, great closet, keeping up with our friends and dropping cash we don't have on stuff we don't need.

The circumstances are very different but the two innate, "reptilian brain" fears remain. Observe any fear that is strong or subtle in your life and you will be able to attribute it to one of these two fear groups.

"I can't tell that person I like them; he or she won't possibly be attracted to me!"

"I can't ask for more money at work, it's not like I'm perfect at my job."
"Who am I to start a business?"

"I can't start a blog – no-one wants to hear what I have to say."

"I don't want to go to that party. I'm not good with new people."

Sound familiar? These are all examples of **I AM NOT ENOUGH**.

What about these:

> *"Money is hard to come by."*

> *"John comes from a better family than I do... I'm kinda embarrassed to introduce him to my parents."*

> *"Better to stick to the career I know than take a risk doing what I really would love to do and go broke."*

> *"Tom makes a lot more money than I do and always has nice things. I feel like he's better than me."*

> *"I won't buy those boots / that laptop / a gym membership — I hate parting with money."*

They are all examples of **I DO NOT HAVE ENOUGH**.

Not all of these examples will come down to fear for everyone. Perhaps you are more of an introvert than a partygoer. Maybe you would rather save for a vacation or a downpayment on an apartment than go shopping for clothes. But only YOU know the true motivation behind statements you make or think. If your soul is stirred with a reason for not doing something that feels right and fair, great. If not, if your decisions leave you feeling insecure, small and unsatisfied, fear has got you wrapped around it's little finger, my friend.

Often, at the highest level, we avoid this introspection. We just want to fit in. We want other people to like and respect us. Our self-esteem is built on what other people like and respect – and that is not necessarily what we really want. But we are afraid to be different.

Over to you.

Applying Principal #1 – Understanding Fear:

1. Think of two instances where fear has prevented you from doing something that might have been harmful. What was the outcome? You can be grateful to your fear for this.
2. Think of three times in your life where you were afraid to do something that you didn't feel ready to do but found the courage and pushed through anyway. What were the positive things that came out of each of these three experiences?
3. Consider one big, current fear. Identify if it is a harmful fear or an ego-based fear – having enough or being enough. If it is a legitimate fear – something that will result in serious harm – thank your fear for keeping you safe. If it is the more likely option, that you are protecting your ego from risk, you can say, "Thanks fear. I can take it from here."

Consider how you can view your current fear as an opportunity to learn, grow, and unearth more of your inner power. That something stirring within you is something good waiting to happen. Your fear is actually showing you what you need to do next.

Lessons From A Leader: James Altucher, Serial Entrepreneur, Thought Leader and Best-Selling Author

Since reading his best selling book "Choose Yourself," James' work has had a profound impact on my life. Side hustlers are ultimately people who choose themselves – people who take their career, the size of their bank account and their impact on the world into their own hands. A former hedge fund manager turned best selling author, podcaster and serial entrepreneur, James has founded or co-founded 20 companies, 17 of which he claims have failed. He has interviewed some of the world's greatest thought leaders and entrepreneurs, including Mark Cuban, Seth Godin, Gary Vaynerchuk, Wayne Dyer and Tim Ferriss for his podcast, "The James Altucher Show." In 2015, he was ranked #4 in the world on LinkedIn's list of most influential people, behind Bill Gates, Richard Branson and Mohamed El-Erian.

Susie: What is the biggest reason for people not to choose themselves, even if they really want to?

James: I can only speak for myself and why it took me so long to realize I could choose myself: wellbeing, financial success, freedom.

From an early age I was taught to obey the rules of society. Rules that were put there largely for good reasons: it's good to stop at stop signs so you don't hurt anyone; it's good to get an education so you can get a job; it's good to own a home so you can have roots and build value while your kids have a consistent place to play.

We've been taught by parents, teachers, bosses – even friends – what is "good" for us. We are also taught by trillions of dollars in marketing what is "good" for us. A 15 trillion dollar mortgage industry. A trillion dollar student loan industry (education is good!), the trillion-dollar economy that needs workers to blindly put fuel into its engines.

This is all fine. But we are not standardized widgets inside a giant robot. Ultimately, we are unique people who have lives to live. We have to develop our own rules that we will adhere to. Rules that will give us wellbeing, happiness and success.

If we don't come up with our own guidelines of what will make us happy, then who will? Well, we know the answer: everyone else will. And it is a guarantee it will not be in our best interests. Not that everyone else is trying to hurt us. It's just that only we know what will be best for us. And often, knowing what will be best for me, is something I had to learn through a lot of trial and error while experimenting with the rules and guidelines of others.

What I want most is wellbeing:

a) Always improving my competence in something I love

b) Always improving my connections with friends and the people I love

c) Always moving towards a sense of freedom. That feeling where no anxiety or stress can bring me down. A sense that I can make the decisions that are good for me and then act on them, whatever they are

The way I build the foundation to do that is to every day try to improve 1 percent (or some tiny, manageable amount), in four areas:

a) Physical health – sleep, eat, move

b) Emotional health – improve my connections with friends and the people I love

c) Mental health – be creative at least once per day

d) Spiritual health – which simply means reminding myself how grateful I am, even in the middle of the most difficult of situations. There are always reasons to be grateful

This sounds so easy! Why don't people always choose to do this? Because for so long, I let others do the choosing for me. And when you do that, the results will never be as good as when I choose for myself.

Susie: What facts do you tell people who still believe in the old world order (safe corporate job, 401K, single paycheck)?

James: I don't like to tell people they are wrong. Nobody listens when you tell them that. We want to believe (I want to believe) that I am right all the time. So I don't tell people when I think they are wrong. I just point out the times I realized I was wrong.

a) 401k. I thought it was good to save away every month in a 401k. Little did I realize the amount of fees and wrong decisions 401k managers constantly make. Nor did I realize that even when the company matches, I would have been far better off investing in myself, or simply having my own cash in the bank rather than waiting until I am near 60.

b) Owning a home. I get it. Many people want "roots." Many people think rent is throwing money out. But you never really own your home. Try missing a mortgage payment, or a property tax, and see how quickly the land from underneath you is taken away. And I learned the hard way that the amount of equity I build is no match for maintenance, renovation, and the thousand other little nicks and expenses that owning a house entails.

Sure, some of the time (and there are a million anecdotes) home ownership works. But as an investment it has all the worst qualities. You would never invest in a company/stock, for instance where:

1. You use 400 percent leverage
2. It can go down as much as 50 percent while you hold it
3. It is totally illiquid (you can't sell it during the times you most NEED to sell it)
4. It requires constant payments to hold onto the investment.

I could go on.

c) Jobs are "safe." Many people go to college thinking that even if they can't do their highest passions in life, they at least can have a "Plan B" that includes a safe job.

Unfortunately, incomes have been going straight down while inflation is going up. The average salary for people ages 18-35 has gone from $36,000 in 1992 to $33,000 now and it's only getting lower.

Meanwhile, the people I know who are doing the best financially have multiple streams of income, do not have a single job, and often the work they do is 100 percent related to their experience and not their education.

"But what about the arts?" I get it. You can learn the arts and humanities in school. And you can have many social experiences in school. But the reality is, with $1.3 trillion in student loan debt (and rising), there are many other, cheaper, safer ways to learn these things. Ways that would be just as enriching, valuable for your future (even more valuable since you will not have debt), and positive socially.

Every society builds its "religion" to keep the masses in check. All I'm saying is: don't reject that religion. Maybe many of its tenets are good for you and your family and the people you love. But always be skeptical. Make sure that if the plane crashes, you are able to put the oxygen mask on your own face first. This is how you help the most people. By helping yourself. By choosing yourself.

Susie: You've started several businesses and have interviewed some of the smartest people on the planet – what are the common shared ideas you all have about choosing yourself?

James: I've interviewed hundreds of successful people: Mark Cuban, Arianna Huffington, mega-movie producer Brian Grazer, Tony Robbins, Wayne Dyer, Barbara Corcoran, football Hall-of-Famer Dan Marino, and on and on.

It's hard to remember every detail from every interview. Just like after I finish a good non-fiction book, I feel really grateful if I can just remember one takeaway. But I will tell you some common things among everyone.

a) Everyone has a mentor. Someone they learned from.

Why is a mentor important? Not to teach you a subject. But to teach you how to learn that subject. Teaching techniques, in every area of life, constantly evolve. So not only does the information in a subject increase but the way one teaches that information is also something that grows and evolves.

If you don't have that teacher then you learn in the same way that people 100 years ago learned. But better to learn quickly the latest learning techniques so the real education can begin.

b) Constant feedback.

When Tony Hawk, 12-time world champion skateboarder and creator of a billion dollars worth of skateboarding video games, skates he gets constant feedback. He either falls or doesn't. Then he repeats.

When Ylon Shwartz, winner of almost $10 million in poker winnings, plays a hand of poker he either makes money or doesn't.

When Andy Weir wrote The Martian, it would either sell books or it wouldn't.

Feedback, and learning from it, is the common theme of success.

c) Attempting to improve every day.

It's not enough to just write every day. You have to learn from everyone around you and try to improve. To be one better. Even in the smallest incremental bit.

Coolio, who wrote the best-selling song of 1995, "Gangsta's Paradise," told me he was writing every day for 17 years before he had a single hit. 17 years!

And along the way, he saw the rap of N.Y.C., Miami, L.A. evolve and grow to use basic beats, then samples of songs, then combine elements of song. And he combined all of that into his own music to be one better and create the greatest hit in the world that year.

This is not all a magic formula. Often we change interests so we don't have 17 years to do ONE thing. That's okay also. We can combine the things we love to create something unique. Ultimately, we are the unique combination of all of our experiences and the things we've learned.

And the goal is not to create the "greatest" X of Y.

The goal is to choose ourselves and, on the day we die, be happy with the choice that we made.

Chapter Three:
How Can I Get Past My Fear?

"We think our fears are precious and special, but they aren't.
WE are precious and special, but our fears are not.
I want us all liberated from the path of fear, for many reasons –
but mostly because it makes for such a damn boring life.
Fear only ever tells you one thing: STOP.
Whereas creativity, courage and inspiration only ever want you to
GO."
~ Elizabeth Gilbert, Author

"Most fear is just bad management of our own mental faculties."
~ Brendon Burchard, Motivational Author

MY hands were sweating. My heart was beating. I looked in the mirror and asked myself, "Why do you always do such crazy shit?" I was not about to jump off a cliff. Nor was I about to do anything illegal. I was about to interview self-made billionaire Sara Blakely, the founder of Spanx, for Marie Claire.

To me, Marie Claire has always been to me one of the coolest publications in the world (even when I was younger and could never afford it). I am not a journalist. I did not go to journalism school. I did not even graduate from college. But somehow with a lot of time, persistence and effort, I managed to secure an interview with one of the world's most successful women for one of the world's most credible publishing houses. I was nervous, on edge, but I got on the phone and the interview happened. I had 42 minutes with one of the smartest business people on the planet. How did it go?

Beautifully. I got lost in what she was saying. I felt like we were old friends. In fact, not only was Sara awesome and inspiring and funny and real, the article was popular and published by her team on the Spanx homepage. She even sent me a bottle of champagne to say thank you.

Similar fears have risen within me on multiple occasions:

- When approaching my school principal about changing the unfair system for kids who had a free school lunch (I was one of them). We were forced to present a very obvious, "my family is really poor" token to the lunch lady in front of all the other kids, which made us feel humiliated.

- Presenting to 20 or more people in boardrooms in New York and Washington D.C. in my sales career.
- During a live television interview with a popular T.V. show in Australia, discussing how to ask for what you want.
- When I saw Jake Gyllenhaal in a downtown New York City restaurant and knew I had to introduce myself (he was lovely).
- Arriving in New York with no network, job opportunities or work authorization and knew I had to present like a boss in interviews to get the job.
- When I quit my lucrative corporate job. I had a plan and a lot of faith and a commitment to work my butt off. But it was still scary.
- Getting married for the second time. I knew it was right this time but still felt scared because of my first experience.
- When I also interviewed Kris Jenner and Kelly Osbourne, also for Marie Claire. They were both very candid and surprisingly cool.

The lesson? You are in the driving seat of your life. Your fear is not. Fear will always accompany you no matter how much you could pay a Park Avenue therapist to eradicate it. But your fears are not in control. You are.

A wonderful thing about life and growth is that the more you take on new challenges – when you let what is greater than fear, your desires, lead – your fear subsides. It has no choice as there is nowhere for it to go but into the background. In the face of action, fear dissolves. This I know for sure. But fear will never evaporate from your life. It can't. I like to think of it this way: "if I had no fear in my life I would have nothing left to do here on earth, would I?"

Remember that at one point in your life you were afraid to have your first kiss. You were afraid to leave home. You were afraid on your first day of school and then your first day of work. But you moved forward anyway. The fear back then was the same as your fear today. The situations just keep getting bigger.

Fear's essence is to protect you (remember that pesky reptilian part of the brain that wants to keep you safe and away from new, potentially dangerous situations)? It pops up 99 percent of the time unrequired.

Your fear never has to rule. In large part it shows you what you need to do next. My friend Molly recently shared with me her two favorite sayings about fear: "It's not fair, but the way things work is that we get the courage to do the things that scare us shitless *after* we do them, not before" and "Courage is not absence of fear but rather the judgment that something else is more important than fear."

Think about this too. There exists a very overused saying: "believe in yourself." Sometimes this is hard, especially in manic moments of self-doubt. So when it comes to making your side hustle your reality you can switch to, "believe in your work." One overworked Thursday you might have had a bad day at the office and come home to an

unhappy side hustle client (this will happen, and it's OK).
You will feel low, drained and sad and ask yourself – why am
I doing all of this? You will want to give up, go to sleep or
watch T.V. until your eyes are square. But it will pass and
you will soon have a great day at the office, a beaming client
and more of a cash injection in your account than you
imagined in a month.

In these moments, ask yourself: what is most
important to you? Pursuing your dream or letting a bad day
(or series of bad days) bring it to an end? Becoming who you
are meant to be or waiting for some criticism from a frenemy
that may never even arrive?

It's time to make it real.

What will you do today and by the end of the week
that will bust through your side hustle blocks? Write that
comedy script? Buy the URL for the food blog you've always
dreamed of starting? Create an email contact list of who to
inform that you're launching a matchmaking service,
personal branding business or life coaching practice?

Take a small step. Today. Give yourself two deadlines:
one 24-hour deadline and one 7-day deadline to take two steps
toward starting or building upon your side hustle.

*"Whenever you have a problem repeat over and over, 'All is well.
Everything is working out for my highest good. Out of this
situation only good will come and I am safe.' This simple
affirmation will work miracles in your life."*
~ Louise Hay

Before I launched my side hustle as a life coach and
writer, I was depressed. Don't get me wrong, for a very long

time I really loved my sales career. I was good at it. I made all my friendships working in advertising. It allowed me, and my husband, to have a very nice lifestyle. I had the most fun of my life traveling, meeting people, learning about cool and innovative online products. I was grateful for all of those things.

But I had learned and mastered everything I wanted to in that career. I did not want to be a Senior Vice President of Sales. I did not want to sell other products in a different company ("same shit, different toilet" as my friend Tal jokes). I was ready to abandon what had become so familiar to me. My heart knew it. I felt my heart beating inside my chest and some days I even felt in pain when I could not see a transition in sight. Poet and philosopher Mark Nepo explains it really well. He says that life is a continuous cycle of "learning, mastery and abandonment."

I knew there was something new for me to learn and master! After half-heartedly doing some interview training as a side business I decided I needed to kick myself in the butt and get a legit side hustle going. I found the website of a NYC life coach and asked if I could take her to lunch to learn a bit about her business. I did the same with another coach. I loved meeting them. They opened up my eyes. Their work was really meaningful to them. And they did it full time! They ran their own schedule (freedom!) and helped people all day. I signed up at New York University as soon as enrollment began and my life-coaching path began.

At around this time I turned 30. This is an age that we refer to in coaching where we transition out of "novice adulthood." That was exactly how I felt. It was time to get real about my life and my life's real work. I did not want a decade to pass and still feel this way (or probably a lot worse). I had also gained weight. I was drinking a lot. I didn't realize it – it happened so slowly over time. Does any of this feel familiar? There are signs that something needs to change when you pay attention.

Once my side hustle was live and kicking – and profitable – I felt a renewed passion for my life. For everything. I even kinda enjoyed my job again! I saw it as a place holder for my "real career." I saw everyone – clients, colleagues, peers – in a new, life-coaching light. I felt lighter. I started introducing myself as a life coach. My corporate clients and peers were psyched for me too! I blended the two worlds however I could.

For example, when the startup I helped build for almost four years was purchased by AOL, I realized AOL also owns The Huffington Post! So whom did I email? Arianna Huffington! And what did she do? Not only was she extremely nice and complimentary of the writing sample I sent her, but she also got an editor to set me up as a contributor on their platform. And who is a prolific contributor in their healthy lifestyle section? Me! That might even be how you heard about me in the first place. Since then, I have interviewed her twice and she has personally shared my work on social media a couple of times.

There are two lessons here:

1. **You have to be resourceful**. Who do you know within your network (including a few degrees of separation) that could be a great connection for you on our entrepreneurial journey?

2. **Important people are more approachable than you realize**. Because people rarely approach them.

My "colleague" Arianna really hooked me up. There are opportunities everywhere if you open your eyes and look. The side hustle really puts you in that positive, go-getting, magnetic zone. With a negative, closed attitude this massive opportunity would never have been seized. And it almost wasn't.

So, let's get down to the nitty gritty.

These are probably the worst things you are thinking can happen when you launch your side hustle:

- You happen to lose some money in set-up costs
- You change your mind about your side hustle idea
- People laugh when you tell them about it
- You don't know what to do or how to start
- You start and then quit
- You never make any money from it
- Your company/boss is not supportive
- You find your passion disappointing
- You aren't good at your side hustle
- Someone says, "I told you so"

Perhaps the worst that can happen is it builds, you quit your job and for whatever reason it is not financially sustainable. SO WHAT? If it does fail, most of the time you can get another job and then reassess. This is especially true if you keep your network alive! Keeping in touch with people is important and when you do, almost nothing in career-land is irreversible.

Remember that people lose their jobs even if they don't pursue a side hustle. Pursuing your hustle will make you feel more empowered and therefore more able to handle life's inevitable challenges. So ask yourself: what is the best that can happen? I guess there is only one way to find out.

Over to you.

Write all your concerns down. But don't stop there. Keep asking yourself: And then what? And then what? To each one. Keep writing. I promise it won't end up with you toothless, living under a bridge.

Secondly, of those concerns, what can you do from the outset to manage, contain or prevent them?

Lessons From A Leader: Alex Cavoulacos, Co-Founder, C.O.O. & Head of Product, The Muse

The Muse is the only online career resource that offers a behind-the-scenes look at job opportunities with hundreds of companies, original career advice from prominent experts, and access to the best coaches to get personalized and private career help. It has helped more than 50 million people with their careers and receives over 8 million visitors a month. Prior to founding The Muse, Alex was a management consultant at McKinsey & Company. She has been named one of Forbes' 30 Under 30 in Media and one of Inc's 15 Women to Watch in Tech.

Susie: You started The Muse when you were very young. What was it that inspired you to take this route?

Alex: Some people know they want to start a company and search for the idea that inspires them. Others are struck with an idea they cannot do anything but pursue. My co-founders and I were so inspired by the opportunity to help people in their careers that we had to start The Muse.

Susie: For many people the biggest block to starting a business is the fear of rejection and/or failure. How did you overcome this?

Alex: We were definitely scared of failure and faced a lot of rejection, day in and day out – and still do. What made it easier was thinking through the worst-case scenario: what if we gave it our all, tried and tried, but didn't make it work, got into debt, moved in with friends or family, and finally realized we had to pull the plug on our dream? Painful? Definitely. But not something we couldn't recover from. If that happened, we'd have to take the first decently paying job we got, pay off our debts and decide what we wanted to do next. Certainly not the outcome we wanted, but by thinking about how bad it could get we realized it was a risk we were willing to take.

Susie: You're the most productive person I know! What keeps you going?

Alex: Hearing from Muse users whose life and careers we have helped is the most inspiring thing and fuels me on tough days. Having that deep connection to our mission and the difference we are making is critical.

Susie: What is your #1 piece of entrepreneurial advice for a beginner?

Alex: Work with co-founders or partners that share the same values and ethics as you; and get industry-standard paperwork sorted out from the beginning. Too many ventures fail because people trust that a verbal agreement will hold, or because difficult conversations are avoided. Starting a company is hard, so face those conversations head out to be sure you've picked the right partner.

Susie: What would you say is the best thing about entrepreneurial life so far?

Alex: Building an incredible team of brilliant, inspiring women and men. Working with them each day in the office makes me a better person and pushes me to grow in ways I couldn't have imagined.

Susie: What is the best piece of business advice you've been given?

Alex: Be yourself. Bring your authentic self to the office and be genuine about your strengths and weaknesses.

Susie: If you could go back and give yourself some advice at the very start of launching your business, what would it be?

Alex: I don't know if I would go back and tell myself anything at the start. There is so much I didn't know, so much for me to learn, but I had endless optimism and energy. I knew that we would figure it out. We had the right team, and we were solving an important problem that could help millions of people.

Chapter Four:
How To Find Your Side Hustle

"Some of the most successful side-giggers I interviewed built businesses that cost very little to start, could be scaled up easily as they grew, fit well with their full-time jobs, took advantage of their own passions and creativity, and most importantly, were incredibly enjoyable.

"You have to love your side business because you'll be working on it at night, on the weekends, and in almost every spare hour you can find."
~ Kimberley Palmer, "The Economy Of You"

Here are some side hustles that I know of:

- Flipping houses
- Proofreading/editing
- Home fashion consulting
- Political blogging
- Creating organic skincare products
- Event planning
- Producing first date hampers for picnics
- Teaching English
- Transportation for the elderly
- Nutrition/wellness coaching
- Teaching budget conscious millennials party planning
- Being a personal organizer
- Teaching people simplified tax preparation
- Designing logos
- Nature photography
- Wedding speech writing
- Teaching others how to double their Instagram following
- Financial planning for recent college graduates
- Triathlon trainer
- Writing romantic/steamy short stories
- Inventing a new brand of coffee
- Options trading
- Creating custom-made bras
- Making organic candles
- Executive business coaching

- Jewelry making
- Personal styling
- Creating high-end bath mats
- Personal shopping
- Running a YouTube cooking channel
- Real estate investing in high growth markets
- Beekeeping/selling honey
- Selling home-made stationery
- Soccer refereeing
- Providing doggy massages for elderly canines
- Private tutoring
- Grant writing
- Offering a high-end hair-extension service
- Doing voiceovers

Some of you might not need this chapter. It might be burningly obvious that you have a novel inside you, or that your future is filled with beautiful gardens to landscape or organic baby clothing to design and create. But some of us need a little help. We know what things interest us but can't identify exactly what our passion might be, let alone get started creating a business out of it.

As I've already said, according to a 2012 Gallup poll, only 13 percent of Americans are engaged, or feel psychologically committed, at work. When I surveyed my blog subscriber list at the end of 2015, I found some alarmingly similar results. Here is what I found:

When asked, "**What scares you the most?**"

- 43.09 percent of you said: "Not fulfilling my potential here on earth."
- 28.73 percent said: "Not knowing what I am good at and being stuck in my day job."

When asked, **"How would I feel if my work situation was exactly the same 12 months from now?"**

- 48.73 percent of you said, "Not good at all."
- 31.16 percent said, "Okay, I guess."
- 17 percent said, "Pretty good" and a mere 3.12 percent of you answered, "Happy. I love my job and it's all I want for now."

The comments said it all:

"Defeated"

"I officially feel stuck and bored"

"I'd need antidepressants"

Finally, to the question, **"How much of my current income (as an employee) would I truly be willing to forgo in order to be my own boss?"**

- 19.50 percent of you said you would give up 30 per cent
- 23.27 percent said you would give up 20 percent

- 28.30 percent said you would give up 10 percent
- 28.93 percent were unwilling to sacrifice any of their salary to go out on their own

I understand that this is somewhat of a loaded question and the way I worded it implies quitting your job altogether. I certainly do not suggest doing this until you have successfully paralleled your hustle with your full time job and it is completely self sustaining.

What's important here are the numbers. A huge number of people are so unhappy with their work situation they would forgo a large portion of their income to pursue their passion.

Here's the good news. And it's important. You are not your job. You are much bigger than and not restricted by whatever your job title says you are – even if you love your current career. In this chapter I am borrowing from a popular piece I wrote for the health and fitness website Greatist, titled Your Job Doesn't Define You. Here's How To Discover What Does.

As a life coach, the number one reason people come to me is because they feel limited – and unfulfilled – by the work they are doing. They come to me for help figuring out their "purpose" or "calling." All day at work they are humming along, looking happy on the surface, but feeling frustrated. They feel bored. They feel inauthentic, which eats away at their self-esteem. As best-selling author Steven Pressfield puts it, they feel like a "shadow version" of themselves. They know that they have the energy, passion, and smarts to do anything – they just don't know what exactly. Or how to begin.

Sadly, no one is going to hand you your passion (plus instructions to bring it to life!) in an envelope. But there are some important questions you can ask yourself to identify what calls to you and ignites your spirit. Getting quiet, going inward, and being honest about what sparks joy within you – and then taking action to actualize it –is very, very powerful. Listening to your inner wisdom and being guided by it brings with it certain magic.

Here are 5 questions you can ask yourself in order to get clear on what your side hustle might be:

1. "What am I doing when I'm slacking off at work?"

My client Dave is a great engineer. When he got an unexpected bonus he spent the entire thing on photography equipment. His weekends are spent taking snaps of Manhattan and Brooklyn. He only follows photographers on Instagram and reads photography blogs and articles online whenever he is bored in work meetings or has a quiet hour or two to spare in the office. In fact, he spends hours at the office researching photography exhibitions and even planned a trip to a European show. His photography passion was undeniable.

When a friend paid him to take artsy photos for his company website, Dave said to me, "Susie is this what dying and going to heaven feels like?" Um... yes! Disclaimer: I certainly do not suggest you slack off at work, but let's face it, for many of us there is a lot of idle time and what we spend that idle time doing could be a great indicator.

2. "What brought me joy as a kid?"

Believe it or not, your passions may evolve and grow, but they never actually change or leave you. When you were very young, what made you happy – playing music, writing stories, helping animals, being captain of a sports team, building stuff? Jack Canfield, motivational speaker and co-author of the "Chicken Soup for the Soul" series, recommends conducting what he calls a "joy review."

Write down times in your life that you felt most happy. Was it when you backpacked through Asia on a shoestring budget? Led the debate team in high school? Trained junior staff at work? Or decorated your past two apartments? Likely, you'll find a common thread throughout those joyful moments. When you see it all on paper, it's easier to connect the dots.

3. "What blogs and books do I love to read?"

Think about the top five websites you peruse once you power up your laptop. For example, I worked with a realtor who spent hours reading recipes in cookbooks, websites, and natural food blogs. He now has a decent following as a food blogger himself and earns a small revenue stream from it. Look at who you follow (aside from friends) on Facebook and Instagram.

4. "What conversation topic never gets boring?"

What subject brings on that, "I could talk about this all day!" feeling? My husband, for example, loves talking about investments – if he had a second job, it would be flipping homes, he always says. It's a total snooze fest for me, but luckily he has a brother and a couple close friends who share his passion.

It's important not only to ask yourself which topics energize you but which people can get excited about them with you. It's critical to nurture relationships where a common passion unites you. Which leads us to...

5. "Who is my tribe?"

Your tribe consists of people who get you. It might not be your colleagues, your college pals, or even your siblings. A close former coworker of mine found her tribe at a popular, local fitness class. When I see her around her tribe, she is the brightest and most energized version of herself. It's awesome!

If you don't have a "tribe" already, you can find one. Use all of the clues above to pinpoint your interest and then locate a group that shares it. Join a book club. Take a cooking class. Learn to code at a local college. Volunteer at an animal shelter. Opportunities and people are everywhere when you open your eyes and look. I found some remarkable tribal pals at New York University, where I spent my Saturdays with people of all ages and professional backgrounds training to become certified life coaches.

Once you have some clarity, you have to take action. Nothing, nothing, nothing changes without action. When I started coaching I was working full-time as an advertising sales director. I thought I wanted to coach people on how to sell. I enjoyed it, but realized that what I love most is coaching people on how to do something else: harness their personal power to gain confidence and pursue their dreams. I know it's possible, especially after having actualized mine.

Ask yourself: what are three things that I can do over the next seven days to bring my passion to life? Then do them. Set up that YouTube account so you can start posting your instructional videos. Tell your friends and colleagues you're available as a Halloween party planner in exchange for a testimonial. Ask the woman you look up to in marketing if you can buy her a latte for 20 minutes of her time. The options are endless.

The following week, do three more. Then three more. And watch what happens. Keep doing this – never stop doing. The results will astound you once you get busy.

Remember: anything good that has ever been created has been the result of small, consistent actions. A few dollars here, a few dollars there adds up to a sweet sum of savings. Smart lunch choices repeated over time result in a healthier body. This is no accident, and self-exploration is no exception. At any moment you can begin the process of going deeper into yourself and bringing the innermost (gorgeous, ready, willing!) part of you to life.

You are not your job. Your job is one part of your multifaceted, potential-filled self. And deep down you know it too. What are you waiting for? As the 13th century Persian poet Rumi wrote, "What you seek is seeking you." Your joy, tribe, and bliss are patiently waiting. They will always be waiting. You just need to act.

Get busy brainstorming!

You just have to pinpoint a passion. Most people have a few, but just choose one, to start, that fits these criteria: You have a talent for it, people want/need it, and you can make money doing it. It can be anything from teaching calligraphy to planning parties to freelancing as a website creator. Don't over-think it! Your business will change over time, so just begin. What are some of your ideas?

Again, think of someone you know who really believes in you. They can be your spouse, best friend, parent, former manager, anyone at all... they don't even have to be in your life (or alive) anymore. It can be a high-school teacher or a coach you once had. My dad died when I was 19 and I think of him a lot and what he would say about the work that I am doing now. Think about what this person who believes in you would think about your new business/creative venture. What would they say/tell you?

Now listen: They are right. Your doubt is not.

Over to you.

Brainstorm 10 potential hustle ideas. Don't think too much, just write – it can be teaching English, selling jewellery on Etsy, peddling your famous cheesecake at the local church – anything. Come up with a minimum of 10 ideas. You won't feel ready but that's the point. We want to get our ideas flowing because this is an action book.

Once you have your 10 ideas, give each a rating in terms of your instinct, your intuition and plausibility. Talk with a friend you trust. Share with this person your 10 ideas.

Ask him or her:
1. These are my ideas. What do you think?
2. What am I most good at here?
3. Is there anything I am missing?

Once you have narrowed your list down to one, ask yourself these questions:
1. Who is doing this already? I.e. your possible competitors or partners.
2. What platform/format are they using to sell their product or service? E.g. In person classes, online courses, brick and mortar stores, cookbooks, consulting.
3. What is their pricing structure?
4. How are they marketing/branding their product or service? How are they communicating with their customer/subscriber base and how frequently? E.g. Weekly/monthly emails containing free tips/recipes.
5. What FREE online resources (or even cheap books) can I use/read to learn more about establishing myself in this niche/industry *before* spending money on courses or licensing?
6. How can I differentiate my offering and brand?

Answering the above questions will really help answer a lot of your initial questions and give you sense of the direction you need to be heading. Think about how your own hustle may fit within the framework of these questions.

Chapter Five:
Why A Vision Board May Help

STILL struggling with unlocking what a passion might be? A vision board event can help! I have held a lot of these – from small gatherings at my home to corporate and non-profit events. It's amazing the stories that come from them – one woman thought she wanted a baby but instead her board was filled with travel images. She wanted to see more of the world first. Another got an idea to create handbags after being drawn to images and locations where she could find materials and create a unique line of her own.

The truth is, many people have trouble pinpointing exactly what it is they want. This makes them feel blocked, stuck and unclear about their goals. Here is an edited version of a piece I wrote for a well-known news site in Australia on how to create a vision board with friends.

Put simply, a vision board is a collage of images, pictures, and affirmations of your dreams, goals (anything that makes you feel happy and inspired) all on one simple A3 board. Some people call them an inspiration board or a dream board. Vision Boards not only work (they help you get clear on what you want and unlock the magical flow of manifestation), but through the power of images we can visualize our future for ourselves – responding and putting on paper the visions that "call" to us.

It is a fabulous way to get specific and put your dreams on paper in a unique (and fun) way. A client of mine put a picture of the Golden Gate Bridge on her vision board last year and two months later received a job transfer to San Francisco.

A friend chose an image of a musician playing the piano and then met and fell in love with a man who played in a local band.

In New York City I hold vision board parties for my clients and as part of my workshops. If you want to host your friends at home this is a wonderfully different way to get together and get a gorgeous result from it. It's a ticket to open the floor to discuss and share your goals and support one another in doing so.

This is all you need to throw a great event at home:

1.   Open-minded friends

Vision board parties feed on group energy. Invite your positive, imaginative and open-minded friends over. Not only will you have a blast, you will create something meaningful together that you can discuss for the entire year (or years) to come. Around 6-8 people is a good group size.

2.   Materials at the ready

A vision board is something you create from scratch – all you need are some magazines (home style, fashion, food, business, family), a poster board (from anywhere), scissors and glue. Tell your friends not to read the magazines. They are a source of inspiration and cutout material only. Your friends can bring their old mags too (as well as an appetizer).

3. A little bit of scene setting

Play some soft or uplifting tunes and light a couple of candles. Make it feel a bit more inspired and Zen-like than usual. No television. No phones (unless it's to play your chill-out playlist). A Zen setting creates an intimate environment that lends itself to a creative and intuitive group mindset.

4. Clear instructions and directions

Not everyone will know how to create a vision board. Explain that it is important not to over-think it. It's simply a matter of creating a collage of images/illustrations and words that "speak" to you. Tear them out of the magazines and arrange them on a page. Tear first, glue later (but everything has to be glued before they leave – no scraps of paper to leave the house).

5. A visualization or a reading

This is not any old night in. Rather than get carried away with talking and drinking, and forget to focus on your boards, insist that people come over at a certain time, sharp. Then read a short visualization or meditation passage to open the evening to get everyone in the same headspace (there are millions, Google "short visualization/presence/meditation passage"). This will ensure that everyone is focused on the present moment and knows why they are there. You can also do a quick round of introductions (if not everyone knows each other) and everyone can set an intention for their board.

6. Collaboration and flow

Encourage your friends to talk about their boards and image choices. Creativity begets creativity and group energy can be powerful and magnetic. Also, remember that the theme/ideas can change while in the process of creating the board. You may think you are creating a board for financial success but along the way focus more on home and family life. Enjoy the 'aha!' moments and talk about them with each other. This is, in fact, one of the highlights of vision board creation – the unexpected desires that surface. Your hustle ideas will flow freely!

7. A little blank space

Tell your friends to leave a little space on their boards for anything they see that might inspire them later. They could even put a radiant, happy picture of themselves in the center. Explain that it is important to keep the vision board in a place where they see it everyday. This is how the law of attraction is multiplied.

It's a lot more fun to share this imaginative and artistic experience with others. And it's a wonderful break from digital distraction. It also brings people together in a uniting and unique way.

Over to you.

Set a date. Grab a group of hustlers, or people you know who just want more from their lives. Then roll up your sleeves and let the festivities (and manifestation magic) begin. What transpires might astonish you!

Tweet me what came up for your hustle @susiemoore!

Lessons From A Leader: Sean Behr, Co-Founder & C.E.O., ZIRX

Sean is an Internet veteran who has helped build wildly successful marketplace businesses in e-commerce (shopping.com, acquired by eBay for approximately $634 million) and advertising (Adap.TV, acquired by AOL for $405 million). Headquartered in San Francisco, ZIRX Mobility Services allows auto manufacturers, dealerships and fleet owners to offer a unique customer experience and manage backend operations more efficiently.

Susie: You started ZIRX in your thirties. What was it that inspired you to take this route?

Sean: Before starting ZIRX, I was an executive at another company and helping to manage and grow that business. But I wasn't creating anything new. As an entrepreneur I've always wanted to create new ideas, new products, and new companies.

Susie: For many people, the building block to starting a business is the fear of rejection and/or failure. How did you overcome this?

Sean: The American game of baseball provides a great lesson in failure and rejection. The best baseball players in the world fail 70 percent of the time when hitting a baseball. When a baseball player fails there is no ongoing gloom; there is no long sense of failure – only another opportunity to hit in the future. I think that's a good analogy for those starting their own business.

Susie: What keeps you going in moments of exhaustion/fatigue and stress?

Sean: A great feeling that I am working on something that can be bigger than me, and that I am surrounded by people who all want the same thing.

Susie: What is your #1 piece of entrepreneurial advice for a beginner?

Sean: Dive in! There has never been a better opportunity to start a business: the costs have never been lower; the risks have never been lower. The opportunity to make money has never been higher. Don't die wondering.

Susie: What would you say is the best thing about entrepreneurial life so far?

Sean: Being an entrepreneur and leader is my natural self-expression. I'm blessed that I get to work on that every day.

Susie: What has been the biggest surprise about entrepreneurial life?

Sean: Even when it's hard (and there will be times when it will be hard) it's still a great ride.

Susie: What is the best business advice you've been given?

Sean: Solve big problems. Whether you are working for a company or starting a business, solve big problems. If you solve a problem for people, they will want to work with you, buy your product or service and likely pay you for it.

Susie: Knowing what you now know, what would you tell yourself at the very start of launching ZIRX?

Sean: I would continually ask myself, "If I could only do one thing today to make the biggest difference in the business, what would it be?" Then work on that...

Susie: What is your #1 productivity hack to have a full business and life?

Sean: Have a system which records all the things you have to do, want to do and wish you could do. Get as much of the stuff in your brain captured somewhere. That leaves you with a freedom to focus on the key things you need or want to accomplish right now.

Susie: What do you feel are the essentials for getting a business up and running on a shoestring budget?

Sean: Get a few customers fast (even free customers). The quickest route is to get your first 3 customers. You will learn so much from your first 3 customers and it will save you a ton of time and energy down the road.

Chapter Six:
Why You'll Never Be "Ready"

"It's a terrible thing, I think, in life to wait until you're ready. I have this feeling now that actually no one is ever ready to do anything. There is almost no such thing as ready. There is only now. And you may as well do it now. Generally speaking, now is as good a time as any."

~ Hugh Laurie

"Amateurs sit and wait for inspiration, the rest of us just get up and go to work."

~Stephen King

"The secret of getting ahead is getting started. The secret of getting started is breaking your complex overwhelming tasks into small manageable tasks, and starting on the first one."

~ Mark Twain

YOU will never, ever, ever be ready to start a side hustle. Like many things in life, conditions are never perfect and it never feels like "the right time" to embark on the adventurous journey of launching something that belongs to you. The sooner you understand this the better. Getting a dog, moving country or getting divorced – I have done them all – and I put them all off at different stages of my life. I needn't have. The result is the same. Getting started just means that you arrive at your destination sooner.

What creeps in here, my friend, with this "being ready" talk is your fear once again. And the only antidote to fear is action. Immediate action.

There is a mistake that we make when we think we are taking action. We think that research, taking a course, going to a million galleries or reading a thousand books is action. Consuming relevant materials matters too of course, but it is not the action that will result in anything apart from your own knowledge. And the purpose of knowledge is to be used. To inspire. To lead you to create. Knowledge, as Napoleon Hill says in "Think and Grow Rich," is only "potential power." You've got to **do the work**.

I'm very guilty here too. I am a huge reader and could get lost in books for an eternity but I still had to write this one. And every single blog post and article that comes from my humble little laptop. I have to write. Not just devour what other writers have created before me. I have to contribute too. That is why we are all here on earth – to make our contribution, however small, and leave the world a little better than how we found it.

I had a client who was passionate about food blogging and could spend four hours on Pinterest creating beautiful boards on baking, spring dishes and party appetizers with table decorations. Fun? Yes. Useful? Maybe. But real work and side-hustlin' this is not. Do not get the two confused. And do not hide behind research or spending thousands of dollars on courses no matter what they promise. A hustle ain't a hustle until it generates money, so don't get caught in hobbyland.

It's a bit like learning to ride a bike by reading all about it and going to a course on it (where there are no actual bikes to ride). You just have to get on it, baby! Get on, fall off, get back on and then learn your own technique. To borrow the words of Aristotle, "For the things we have to learn before we can do them, we learn by doing them."

Getting started is scary. I know this. This is what I tell people who panic the moment the time comes to pull the trigger: get on the bike. It's not about you. You were put on this earth for a greater purpose than the one you are fulfilling – otherwise a side hustle would not ignite your spirit and call to your heart.

We all have a purpose and when we follow what drives our beautiful desires and dreams we are getting closer to it. Your gifts, if you can teach, paint, sell, sing, design, screen write, cook, inspire others, train dogs – whatever you have been blessed with the talent for doing – exists to serve the world, not you and your ego.

Stop obsessing over whether you are good or worthy enough – just show us what you got! When you give your all to what you love to do and surrender the outcome, you kinda have it all figured out. I heard a psychologist say once that even mild forms of unhappiness evolve from too much self-interest. With too much focus on the self we lose the meaning and understanding of what life is for – to use our special gifts and talents to make a positive impact on the lives of others.

Remember that your life is part of a much larger whole. It is your job only to figure out what your role is and then to get busy. Don't ask, "What do I want?" but rather, "How best can I contribute?" Let this be the mantra behind your side hustle if you need one. You have something big to contribute and you just know it, don't you? All you have to do is believe in your work, your contribution. You have something great to offer the world! The understanding that it is not about you, it is about your offering, is really very reassuring. We just have to get out of our own way.

Over to you.

1.   Schedule time.

Clear a block of at least 4 hours a week (2 hour chunks if you work better in smaller bursts) to get your side hustle action going. Like an appointment or important meeting, this time is neither changeable nor negotiable. Schedule it! Put it in your calendar! Unless someone dies this is your time to get busy (and not research – write/create/do). Do not answer the door. Ignore the fire in the kitchen. Your hustlin' time is more important. The beauty is, often these chunks of time grow from 2 hours to 3-4 without us even knowing the time passes. This is called being in the flow.

2. No excuses.

As you get ready to work and whenever you
consider your side hustle, guard your mind (more on this to
come later). Every time a negative thought creeps in to tell
you achieving your goal is not possible, or to hinder you
from getting started, release it immediately and consciously.
You also might want to limit your time around non-believers
too, people who are cynical about anything outside of a 9-5
job. They will say things like, "Come on, it's Sunday, time for
a movie/coffee/beer." Success takes sacrifice. You won't
regret it later. Remember only results matter! **Excuses
don't.**

3. Remove distractions.

Keep your phone at bay. Shut down all social media
and turn off your laptop notifications. Make yourself
unavailable for anything or anyone during your hustle time.
As I write this, my mail is switched off, as is the messenger
on my laptop, which normally pops up anytime there is a
text from a friend. Off, off, off. The silence is your friend.
Also, while I write this book I have unsubscribed from
almost everything that is in my "self-help/productivity/kick-
ass in life" genre. And I follow a lot of people! I was always
looking at Instagram seeing what they were up to, what they
were promoting and who with. I have given myself a self-
help book hiatus. As a total junkie this was hard but for a
couple of months I have committed to fiction only so I can
channel what is inside of me and not be diverted by new
ideas or topics. I have 3-4 books already waiting for me. But

until I write THE END, all my mentors and contemporaries are on pause. They might have run for office and I wouldn't even know. My priority is my book. Side note: this lack of distraction kinda feels good. I may not re-subscribe to a lot of online info...

4. Set a deadline.

Us life coaches are ruthless about deadlines. They are crucial. What does success look like for you and your hustle? Start with the end in mind and give yourself a clear, achievable and realistic deadline to make it happen (e.g., by July 31, 12p.m. EST, I will have finished my novel). Break it up into small, bite-size deadlines, too, to make yourself accountable along the way. Say your novel is 12 chapters. You have 6 months. So that is 2 chapters per month. 1 every 2 weeks. What are you waiting for? 2029? Remember this too: until you launch this project there is no room for another project/idea/inspiration to surface. Get this one done by your deadline and get excited about what's next! The next idea will come, I promise.

5. Enjoy the process!

This all sounds very serious I know. But it's meant to be fun (most of the time, anyway). When we are in the process of doing we are at our most calm, engaged and creative. Be present and enjoy the flow of your talents as you express them. I love to write but I hate updating my website and managing the software system that launches my online courses and weekly newsletters. I outsource most of it but I still need to have a strong understanding of it, so in my moments of frustration I come back to my why. Why does it matter? Hmmm... No website? No courses? No infrastructure? When I first started my business (as a hustle) it wouldn't have mattered, but removing all of this now would kill the momentum. You take the rough with the smooth.

6. Celebrate!

This is my favorite part. You have to celebrate small wins along the way. When you have had one month of applied activity towards your goal, treat yourself! A massage, new motivating book or glass of champagne will inspire you to keep going. I love getting a manicure after a particularly satisfying day of writing – or trying a new restaurant with my husband. Remember, it's about the journey, so season that journey with some enjoyable shit.

Over to you.

Feeling inspired? Get started! I'll wait.

Lessons From A Leader: Jason Wachob, Co-Founder & C.E.O., mindbodygreen

Jason is the C.E.O. of mindbodygreen and the author of "WELLth: How I Learned to Build a Life, Not a Resume." He has been featured in The New York Times, Entrepreneur, Fast Company and Vogue. mindbodygreen is a lifestyle media brand dedicated to inspiring you to live your best life and receives more than 10 million visitors a month. I am forever grateful to Jason, his wife Colleen and the team at mindbodygreen for allowing me to write for them as I first started out, which ultimately gave me the confidence to know I could make it in the field that I love.

Susie: You started mindbodygreen in your thirties. What was it that inspired you to take this route?

Jason: I was running another company and trying to raise capital when I discovered I had two extruded discs in my lower back pressing on my sciatic nerve. I could barely walk and almost had back surgery. Looking back, it was probably related to an old college basketball injury combined with stress and the fact that I was flying almost 100,000 miles a year. Being 6'7" and scrunched into airline seats didn't help. One doctor told me that yoga might be a way to avoid surgery. So I started practicing yoga daily, and was very surprised that I loved it. From there, I got interested in a more holistic lifestyle. I ate organic and ditched toxic household products. I began to meditate. I started a gratitude practice. And after just a few months, I completely healed my back (without surgery). It was a real awakening for me. I realized that health wasn't about weight loss or looking good – it was a blend of how we treated our minds, bodies, and the environment. It was also the inspiration for starting mindbodygreen.

Susie: How did you overcome the fear of rejection and/or failure?

Jason: I had started and been part of early stage startups that didn't work so I knew that it wasn't the end of the world [if I failed]. I also lost my father suddenly to a heart attack when I was just 19 years old. When you lose a parent when you're young, it's devastating but then you make it through it. Things like failure or rejection don't seem like a big deal when you've experienced that type of grief. Malcolm Gladwell has some interesting thoughts on this in his great book, "David and Goliath."

Susie: What keeps you going?

Jason: Pure passion. I absolutely love the mission of mindbodygreen. I believe as an entrepreneur everyone at some time or another faces a "dark night of the soul" moment (or moments) when you've had enough and are ready to throw in the towel. For me it's passion that always keeps me going.

Susie: What is your #1 piece of entrepreneurial advice?

Jason: Only do something you're passionate about. If you're not passionate about it, odds are you'll give up when things get ugly or take twice as long as you think they will. It took three years with mindbodygreen before we knew we had a business. Three years of no salary for me while working full time, and three years of nights and weekend work for my co-founders Tim and Carver. Most would have given up.

Susie: What is the best piece of business advice you have been given?

Jason: I'm still waiting on this one! I read a lot and take bits and pieces from books. A recent book that really resonated with me was, "Everything I Know About Business I Learned From the Grateful Dead" [by Barry Barnes]. I'd also add that some of my most valuable lessons in business have come from basketball.

Susie: With the benefit of hindsight, what advice would you give yourself when starting out?

Jason: "There's a light at the end of the tunnel!" Even though I believe this to be true, it's not always easy believing when you're so caught up in the day-to-day of trying to grow a business from scratch.

Susie: What is your #1 productivity hack for a full life and business?

Jason: Meditation has been game changing for me. It helps me with stress, creativity and focus.

Susie: Many people don't start a business because they feel that a large sum of capital is needed to get things going. What are the essentials for getting a business up and running on a shoestring budget?

Jason: I'm a huge believer in bootstrapping and not raising capital until you are 100 percent certain you know how and are ready to scale. Bootstrapping forces you to focus on building a brand and a great product and finding creative ways to grow revenue – the essentials of a strong business. You need to learn how to grow without throwing money at growth. You'd be surprised how far you can go with so little capital. We started mindbodygreen with nothing (I think Tim, Carver and I pooled together $5k in 2007). The only essential you need to start a business is passion. You can always find capital, you can always find a market, but if you don't have passion then you're in trouble.

Chapter Seven:
How Do I Find The Time?

"Focus on being productive instead of being busy."
~ *Tim Ferriss, Author of "The 4-Hour Workweek"*

"Have you ever rented a video or film that you've already seen?...
Get a fucking life!"
~ *Tony Robbins, Author & Personal Development Legend*

"Insulate yourself from distractions."
~ *Jeff Walker, Author*

"BUT how do I find the time??" I hear you ask.

It varies depending on the hustle, but you can start your side hustle with just a few hours a week. Fun fact: The movie "Pitch Perfect" and "Fifty Shades of Grey," the novel, were largely written on trains – while Kay Cannon and E.L. James were commuting to work. "Pitch Perfect" grossed more than $65 million in 2012 and "Fifty Shades" $95 million in 2013 (E.L. James topped the Forbes list that year as the #1 highest earning author).

Hmmm... do you really need those hours playing Candy Crush or stalking people on social media? Do you really need to binge on "Silicon Valley?" Guess what? None of that will help you retire in Maui!

It's not about time; it's about priorities. We all have 24 hours in a day. That said, I'm sharing with you my ultimate productivity hacks – how to get more done in less time. These are useful whether or not you have a side hustle – they are killer timesaving tips that can help everyone!

1. Commute wisely

Here is what I do. In the mornings I take a few minutes to consciously write (with intention) in my 5-minute journal. If I can help it, I don't check my email or social media until I am out the door. Here is why:

-       2 minutes waiting for elevator
-       2-3 minute wait for subway
-       12-minute subway ride
-       3-minute wait for coffee
-       1-minute wait for the next elevator

= 21 minutes of social media time to check while idle/waiting, if you must. Use this time to check your Instagram, Facebook and Twitter feed (1-2 mins each) and then respond to any overnight texts or emails = 15 mins. Perfect! Also, checking email often causes me stress and I don't want to think about the needs of other people the first second I wake up. I want to think about my needs and my journal allows me to do just that.

I enjoy social media as much as the next person and use it to a certain degree in my business. However, a 2015 Adweek study showed that users spend an average of 1.72 hours on social media a day! Let's be honest, an hour and 43 minutes a day spent watching stupid videos and comparing our lives to others is a little sad.

2. Use wait time well

As with the above, if I am waiting in line at the grocery store, in Starbucks, waiting for my nails to dry or for a friend to arrive at brunch I use those minutes to either catch up on my reading, take some notes for an upcoming product launch, start a blog post/article, shoot my sisters a text to say hi or respond to some less-urgent emails. Most people have up to 1 hour idle wait time on an average day – more if you have an appointment at a hairstylist, doctor or vet. It adds up! You might just have uncovered the 7 or more hours you need to get the day-to-day stuff done, leaving you more time to work on your hustle.

Think about it. Because you have disputed and corrected that phone/medical bill via a phone call while walking to the supermarket (I like to call AT&T while walking/doing – there is so much on hold time) and responded to that business contact while waiting in line, you now have 30 free minutes to spend in your evening to do some real work on your business. Do the stuff on the fly that can be done on the fly. Conserve your hours using these little pockets of wait or commute time to give you freedom and clear your head to do your real work at home.

3.   Say no, no, no

No is one of my favorite words. You wanna know why it's so magical? Because when you say no to what doesn't serve you, you say YES to yourself (and the things that serve you). Mastering the art of saying no has been life changing for me. I call "No" the new black. Time is a completely nonrenewable resource, and when used and planned correctly, it's our friend, not our enemy. (How often do we hear people say, "I don't have time?" That is enemy-talk.)

When there are many things going on, breathe, take a moment, and let your intuition decide what makes most sense. A run or brunch? Drinks with a friend or two hours spent on your blog? Before accepting an invitation, think, "Am I genuinely excited or looking forward to this?" If yes, go for it! If you're not certain, say you will let the person know. If not, politely decline. A simple, "Thank you so much for the invite, so sorry I can't make it" will suffice. Do it. It gets easier with time, I promise. We all have 24 hours in a day – including Beyoncé – you know the best ways to spend yours.

If you say no to one social dinner/drinks a week plus one meeting a week – including commute time each way – what is that, 8-9 hours? That is the equivalent of a whole workday on your hustle! Don't attend things purely out of the fear of missing out (FOMO). Respect your schedule and people will respect you for it.

Another option is to catch up with friends all at once. When my side hustle really started to grow, I was not only working a very busy job but I was traveling a lot for work too. I felt like I was constantly letting people down by turning down plans and not being very active on the social scene. So I held some parties! This allows a lot of people to come together at once. Inviting a group of people into your home also allows you to connect others, a key to building awesome, lasting relationships. Reserve a Friday or Saturday night, tell your friends to come over and bring a bottle. Serve some simple appetizers, play some cool tunes – and boom! You've caught up with everyone. And everyone gets to meet new people. And there is nothing as lovely and intimate as a house party. The few hours spent in prep and tidying are a good investment.

4. Run errands on work time (if you can)

This is a bit of a controversial one and I recommend using discretion, but I see a lot of people do this really successfully. No one (well no one I have ever met) is busy every minute of the workday. They might say they are or look like they are but there are a lot of wasted minutes in every day, I can assure you. Think about Friday afternoons at 4p.m. or an idle Wednesday when the office is quiet and your to-do list is done. Don't resort to Facebook or Instagram or your favorite shopping site. Do some easy, quick errands, which frees up hustle time later.

Here are some things you can do on your down time at work:

- Pay any non-automated bills online
- Buy home essentials on Amazon
- Book your dog or cat in for the vet
- Visit doctor/dentist (they're hard to book after hours)
- Go to the post office
- Go to the bank
- Plan what to cook that evening
- Make appointments with hairdresser, accountant, etc.

Some people go to the gym or take a spin class during their lunch hour. Great idea! Then from 5 or 6 p.m., depending on your profession, the evening is yours. Doing all of this, when possible, on work time can save hundreds of hours over time for side hustle action after work and on the weekends.

5. Make phone calls on the go

Who do you need to call? Do it while moving! I catch up with friends on the phone while walking to and from the subway, unloading my dishwasher, buying stuff at Walgreens or walking my dog. I carry my headset everywhere so I can make calls or listen to podcasts. Side note: Listen to inspirational podcasts that keep you focused and motivated – you'll find my favorites at the back of this book.

6.   Unsubscribe

If you are anything like me you get a lot of junk email from airlines, beauty/retail sites, news sites etc. Just do yourself a favor and lose 90 percent of it. Unless you live to hear from that person or company, just clean out your inbox. Fewer distractions that clutter your inbox really help. When it comes to important emails, it can be more efficient to pick up the phone and respond to people than reply and create a back and forth. Also, when we're in a rush, this can come across in email in a blunt tone – a phone call avoids this.

7.   Drop something

In 2014, I heard Arianna Huffington speak at her *Thrive* conference in New York. She said something that astounded many in the audience: "One of the best ways to complete a project is to drop it." Ha! What a brilliant idea. She said some projects on her "to-do" list were things like learn to ski and learn German. But she decided to just drop them altogether. Just like that! What an awesome idea (and relief).

8.   Skip stuff

It's OK to give yourself permission to miss something – a workout, book club, whatever is regularly scheduled in your calendar every so often. Success does take some sacrifice so give yourself a little break. You will be there next time!

9. Watch television when doing the mindless stuff

I admit it might be impossible to completely give up my favorite shows so I recommend using T.V. time to do stuff that needs to get done but requires very little brainpower. For example, I respond to people that I cannot help and refer them to people who can while I am watching Bravo. And, I'll say it again, don't binge watch!

10. Outsource

Outsourcing has been a huge time saver for me. I outsource tasks such as researching someone I am about to interview to website updates to basic bookkeeping. It allows you to delegate tasks that are an inefficient use of your time – and often at a very reasonable price.

11. Get to know your flow

On my best days, I book nothing before noon apart from writing time. I try to not even open any email accounts if I can avoid it. If something urgent happens I will get a phone call. The morning is when I'm like a supercharged version of myself. I can write 2,000-3,000 words on a good morning. I could never do this after 4p.m. when I'm an uncreative robot.

Figure out your rhythm – when you are the best version of yourself. If you are like me, use your mornings. Some people rock out at night. Use your best brain for your most important work. When I still had my full-time job, I would get up early and pitch 5 ideas to my editors before 6.30 a.m. I would write a blog post (or half a blog post). I would set up important side hustle meetings. Use your most productive hours for your hustle. There is no way I would let a workout, a non-urgent email from my boss or a sink full of dirty wine glasses get in the way of my most important producing time.

I have read from many sources that we have a maximum of 3-4 "good" hours in the day to produce, to be energized, to be at the top of our game. Scheduling our day to maximize these hours for our hustle makes all the difference. There are other moments that pop up in life too, like a Sunday at 3 p.m. when you find yourself a little bored or restless and unable to concentrate. Before you succumb to Facebook or scrolling your contacts for someone to call, think, "What do I feel I never have time to do that I could use this time for?" I like to use it to write thank you cards or clean out my bathroom drawers. Getting this stuff done not only feels good but frees space for more hustle time in the following days.

Steven Covey, author of the bestselling book, "The 7 Habits of Highly Effective People," says something I live by and quote often: "Don't prioritize your schedule, schedule your priorities."

Here are some other top hacks I've learned from fellow entrepreneur friends:

- When on the phone, walk around, tidy up, empty fridge, fold the laundry
- Turn off all social media notifications on your phone and laptop
- Plan the next day's outfit on your commute home
- When waiting for someone (in person or on the phone), write a to-do list or respond to old emails and texts
- Do squats while drying your hair/brushing your teeth
- Get a manicure or go for a walk with a friend, (double-up your pampering and fitness with friendship catch-ups)
- Catch up on motivational podcasts while running errands such as dry-cleaning, going to the bank, pharmacy or to a workout class!
- Skype loved ones while you are cooking
- Obey the two-minute rule: if you can do it in 2 mins do it on the spot! This prevents a mammoth to-do list build up
- Every Sunday night, spend 4 minutes planning the week ahead

Over to you.

Look at your calendar for next week and find three things you can skip – a social event you don't really want to go to, a workout class you can live without, an errand you can do quickly during work time. Cancel cancel cancel! You've just found yourself some extra hustle time.

Lessons From A Leader: Rupa Mehta, Author and Founder, Nalini Method and NaliniKIDS

Rupa Mehta is a teacher, entrepreneur, fitness expert and creator of the Nalini Method. She is the author of "The Nalini Method: 7 Workouts for 7 Moods" and founder of the non-profit organization, NaliniKIDS. Her wellness philosophy – rooted in an understanding that true health comes from being emotionally and physically fit – was developed after working with clients in her New York fitness studios. She has been featured in Vogue, InStyle, The New York Times and The Huffington Post.

Susie: You had a corporate job working in the publishing sector. What compelled you to go out on your own and start Nalini Method?

Rupa: I was at a crossroads in my twenties, debating between moving back to my comforting hometown in Virginia or staying in New York, pursuing my adventurous side and passion. The thing that kept ringing in my ears was, "Teach, teach, teach." It was definitely a risky venture but I wanted something I could jump into with both feet, knowing I was following my heart. Nalini Method was built from the desire for a home base in a big city; a studio that clients could call "home." I knew I couldn't live without teaching in my life, so I built a business that combined my love of home, teaching and fitness.

Susie: What advice would you give to someone looking to become an entrepreneur in the health and wellness space?

Rupa: First of all, you should really love health and wellness and know why. It sounds obvious but once you pick the field in which to commit you have to meditate on what job you'd really like. Do you love taking classes? You might be a good candidate to open your own studio or develop a new class, but you also may contribute best as a writer or blogger in the wellness sphere, building communities. Loving teaching doesn't necessarily mean loving running a business. Being an instructor might be your calling, but you may need to be part of a staff that runs the logistics outside the classroom. In short, find an aspect of the health and wellness space that you really connect to and run with it. And then the key is to work hard and work smart.

Susie: What have been some of the biggest surprises along this entrepreneurial path?

Rupa: The community building; the surprise of meeting people you never thought you might connect with who end up being incredible assets and influencers. I will always take a meeting and meet a new person. Support comes from unexpected places and I am always interested in going out of my comfort zone. I think of the whole world as my community now.

Susie: Nalini Method has really loyal clients. What do you feel is the key to creating loyalty and building a returning client base?

Rupa: Honestly, I think people come back because they're achieving their personal and physical goals. When clients have a space in which they can disconnect and prioritize balance or self-care, they are able to focus and achieve the goals they've set. But it's a two way street: people feel loyal to the studio because my staff and I feel loyal to their needs. I know I wouldn't have a class without them, so I always go the extra mile when it comes to personal attention either in class or out.

Susie: What advice would you go back and give yourself at the start of launching your business?

Rupa: I don't think I have advice I would wish upon my younger self. I saw a sign the other day (while stuck in traffic no less) that said, "Relax. You'll get there when you get there." Advice and mentors are of course huge assets along the way, but I wouldn't have done anything differently, and I think "younger Rupa" should just enjoy the ride!

Susie: What is the best thing about running your own business?

Rupa: I'm proud of the team, community and schedule I've built. I learn so much from those around me that even though I do technically run my own business, I can feel like I have several bosses throughout the workweek. Teaching connects me to people in a very intimate and eye-opening way, and on days when I feel very small (I'm only 5 feet tall, after all!) I feel less alone in the world. The student always ends up teaching me as well, and I am grateful that my business allows me to be a student, day in and day out.

Susie: You also started NaliniKIDS to teach kids the value of emotional and physical fitness. How has it impacted your entrepreneurial journey?

Rupa: I have learned so much from teaching adults over the last 17 years but when I began engaging with kids, I realized I was learning very different and often broader lessons. Kids at this age (K-8) are figuring out their identity and are very impressionable. My team trains teachers to help kids connect life skills, like owning their moods and feelings, to the subjects they are learning in school. One of the most exciting developments over the last couple years is the way that NaliniKIDS has influenced Nalini Method – the two elements work in tandem, making me a better teacher for both adults and kids.

Chapter Eight:
What Is The Worst That Could Happen If I Pursue What I Love?

"Adversities, no matter what they are, simply don't hit us as hard as we think they will. Our fear of consequences is always worse than the consequences themselves."
~Shawn Achor, Happiness Researcher

An email exchange from my days as an employee

Subject: Today

Email Body:
Good morning. Sorry but I need to take a personal day today. I have a 2.30 p.m. meeting, which I have just rescheduled for Thursday. I also have email access and will be aware if anything happens with X client. If you need anything urgent, please call my cell.

See you tomorrow.

Warmly,

Susie

Response: "No worries. See you tomorrow, Susie!"

WELL, well, well. Look what happens when you take a day off work. Nothing. Surprisingly for me that day, no one died. Funnily enough it also did not make the 6p.m. news. Matt Lauer didn't call me for an interview and the guy from Dateline didn't show up on my doorstep with his camera crew.

Let's get real for a minute here. Just say you wanted to take one or two days off work to do some research on your side hustle, bang out some meetings (with the bank, a blogger you want to meet, the designer who is working on your logo), or to finally complete your book (Cheryl Strayed went to the woods for three weeks to complete her bestselling book, "Wild," even though she had small children), no one else's life is going to drastically change.

And sometimes you need to squeeze in some time off. I took a vacation day when I interviewed Kris Jenner, for example. I did not want to risk an urgent mandatory meeting from my boss to interrupt our call. Or a last minute client request to ruin a meeting that took me ages to schedule.

So many people think: Time off? No way! Not me, I can't. But even the President of the United States takes time off. Sometimes when we fear something it seems more serious than it is. What we think *might* happen is often so far removed from reality.

A couple years ago I met someone who was proud of the fact that he never takes time off work. I spoke about a holiday I was planning. "I could never take that much time off," he said. He worked at LinkedIn. I asked him why not. He did not seem to have a specific reason, he just told me that he was "working on some important projects." I wanted to tell him that I was sure some time off would help him relax and refuel and that his colleagues would probably cover his work responsibilities while he was away. Plus, "important projects" never stop coming.

I understand that in some cases taking a day or two off can be difficult. But it is very likely your employer will forget that time off in a week or two's time – and it could have a lifelong impact on your business. Sometimes we need a bit of perspective to help us move forward.

What can this one fear of time off work teach us about how we catastrophize so much in our lives? So you start your side hustle and it takes longer to get off the ground than you hoped... So what? Maybe some set-up costs are a little more than you hoped. So what? You are learning! Say you don't have a ton of traffic in your first week to your new, beautiful website (you won't). Say the editor at Esquire or Cosmopolitan rejects your submission (I have been rejected well over 200 times). SO WHAT?

"So what?" is one of my favorite questions that I ask myself for perspective. I'm a very impatient person. It's a rough virtue, I like to think. I was always in a hurry to succeed and wanted a booming business yesterday. But success takes time. Get to know this now. That is why the side hustle is so killer... it builds over time while you are working.

Recently, I started reading the very popular novel, "A Little Life." As I write this it is up for the Booker Prize. Author Hanya Yanagihara wrote it over 18 months while working full-time as deputy editor of T: The New York Times Style Magazine. This was no mean feat or lazy side hustle application on her part. It's amazing what can happen when you apply yourself.

Thomas Edison said, "If we did all the things we are capable of, we would literally astound ourselves." What would happen if you applied an hour a day to your side hustle? Two hours? Five days a week? What is the best that can happen? Look at Hanya. I don't think she was getting wasted at too many bottomless brunches last year. Heck, your side hustle can even save you money when you think about the socializing it prevents you from doing. You are making money rather than spending it.

Remember this: It's a side hustle! You are still busy with a job that pays the bills. But this is not an excuse to go slow or to put if off. There is an old Chinese proverb that I love: "The best time to plant a tree was 20 years ago. The second best time is today." The future is created in the present moment. Do it now, do it now, do it now.

Over to you.

What can you do you today, *right now* (however small) that will benefit your side hustle? Make it happen.

Lessons From A Leader: Mary Keane-Dawson, Managing Director, Neo@Ogilvy U.K. and Founder, How She Made It

Mary is a serial entrepreneur who has founded and fostered a number of initiatives, including How She Made It, an exclusive community of ambitious, talented and successful businesswomen. She is currently the Managing Director of Advertising Agency Neo@Ogilvy in London and a board member of London Tech Advocates, an initiative created by the Mayor of London.

Susie: You're a serial entrepreneur who has also held some very senior corporate roles. Have you followed a career plan to achieve as much as you have?

Mary: Not a plan, more of an objective/goal driven strategy. Every time I reached my goal, and often when I have been traveling between goals, I have had an eye on the next peak I want to climb.

Susie: How have you overcome any fears of rejection or failure?

Mary: It sounds glib but you have to learn that people respect you because you TRY, even if you don't make it work the first, second or even third time. People who try are always in demand, and opportunity, in my experience, is more likely to seek out a trier over a thinker any day of the week. You have to be intrinsically motivated by curiosity, as well as the desire for material wealth, status and respect. It's important that your psychological needs are satisfied as much as you material needs. [Abraham] Maslow's hierarchy of needs is a good reference for this.

Susie: You juggle a lot in your work and home life (Mom, Board Member, Founder of How She Made It, Philanthropist). What keeps you going in moments of exhaustion/fatigue and stress?

Mary: Meditation. It's as important to empty your mind as it is to be fully in the present, at least once a day. By doing so you reboot and that allows you to reset and revisit your priorities on a daily basis.

Susie: What is your #1 piece of entrepreneurial advice for a beginner?

Mary: Seek out like-minded people to support and advise you. It's amazing (and very satisfying) to experience how helpful people will be in acting as sounding boards, early stage investors, networkers and collaborators as your ideas become a viable business.

Susie: What is the best piece of business advice you have been given?

Mary: Approach business problems from the constructive perspective. Think, "How can I make this work better?" rather than, "Well, that didn't work, so better pack it in..." There are always plenty of reasons not to do something, to give up, go back to the desk job. Approaching issues from the destructive perspective will guarantee that you fail.

Susie: If you could go back and tell yourself something at the very start of your diverse career, what would it be?

Mary: You're a hell of a lot better at making things happen than you realize. Don't seek the approval of others, seek their support.

Susie: What do you feel are the essentials for getting a business up and running on a budget?

Mary: Find your customer, get to know them, and then get them to buy into your prototype/service offering at the earliest possible point in time. That way you bring your customer on the journey with you: they will be your collaborator and enable you to develop your product/proposition as the very best solution for their needs. They'll also finance it.

Susie: What is your #1 productivity hack to have a full life and business?

Mary: Go to bed by 10p.m. and get up at 6a.m. every weekday and always take an hour out of your day to do some exercise/meditation/relaxation or have me time. It has a massive impact on your ability to produce great quality thinking, planning, actions, advice and work.

Chapter Nine:
A Killer Way To Sell Without Being A Sleaze

"If you would take, you must first give."
~ Lao Tzu

REMEMBER, unless you're making sales, your side hustle is a hobby. Sales can be seen as a dirty word but there is no business without cash flow. If you take anything away from this section let it be to position your product or service as valuable to the other person. And before you ask for anything, you need to be a giver of value. A great way to do this is to write. Believe me, you don't have to be a perfect writer – or even a great writer. But writing can grow your business more quickly than almost anything else. Sharing your ideas and tips and information is a wonderful free way to get people to know about you.

I wrote a lot for free and built a small audience before I asked to get paid as a coach or writer. A wise man, Gerd Leonhard taught me many years ago that attention is the most important currency. He said, "don't ask who pays but who pays attention." Writing is an incredible way of checking the pulse on exactly who is paying attention to exactly what.

To show you how simple it is, here is an example of a pitch email I wrote to an editor – I keep it simple. Feel free to use it!

Hope you are well, Jenny!

I am a writer for The Huffington Post and MindBodyGreen (as well as others).

My author pages are here:

http://www.huffingtonpost.com/susie-moore/
http://www.mindbodygreen.com/wc/susie-moore

I am working on an article regarding 10 Reasons Why Courthouse Weddings Are Kick-Ass – The Best Modern Option. I am sharing my wedding experience at City Hall New York – why it was one of the greatest decisions of my life and the best way to start our marriage in our twenties.

Not only are these ceremonies easy, inexpensive and romantic (as it is just you and your beloved) – a surprising amount of celebrities do it: Matt Damon, Jessica Alba, Keira Knightley, even Marilyn Monroe and Joe DiMaggio.

Weddings are a great source of stress, family strain and debt. Courthouse weddings negate all this. You are just as married with a lot less worry, more time to plan a honeymoon (and where to live), plus money in the bank to enjoy for more lasting things! I believe your audience would find great value in this piece.

I hope you find this story compelling and I look forward to hearing from you, Jenny!

Many thanks
Susie

There are 2 things here that I often repeat when pitching a story (or anything else for that matter):

1. Keep it personal – people love to connect on a human level and we all love stories. Human beings are wired to absorb and soak in stories.

Have you noticed how all great speakers often start with a story? Use your own.

2. I speak about bringing value to the audience. I talk about being "in my twenties" and that the audience, most likely on a budget, can get "great value" from my tips. For this editor and her team who need fresh, daily posts, I am offering interesting and relevant content. I did not say how it was my lifelong dream to be published by this great magazine (although it has been one of my goals for a long time). Or anything about what was in it for me.

Side note: this was published the week Kim and Kanye got married. You are likely to get a higher success rate when you pitch ideas that are current and topical!

The real success comes in the follow-up. I followed up with this editor 7+ times, along with many others who never responded. This means that in order to get published once, I sent around 50 emails. In the end the partnership I created with this publication resulted in 20+ paid articles in just a few months and gave me access to interview an array of celebrities. It also gave me leverage to write for more publications. Start small. Dream big. Don't take no for an answer.

In fact, the lovely Sara Blakely told me that "no means nothing." She told me that people ripped up her business card in her face. Interviewing her was such a pleasure and an eye-opening exercise. We often think successful people had it easier than us until we learn how much failure and adversity they endured. People are way more reachable than you think once you cast the net wide and remain consistent. Getting paid by a large and prestigious publishing house also massively boosted my confidence. I felt like a real writer – hell, I was a real writer! And it became increasingly clear that there are way fewer limits than we think there are – no matter how many writer/artist/freelance friends you have who say there is "no work out there."

You have to position yourself as a professional

There is a huge advantage for people who know how to talk about, package and position their offering (whatever it may be) and ask for what they want – a job, an introduction, a new client, an opportunity. The people who get hired, get the gig, land the deal are schooled in something else – simple asking savvy. Sure they are huge providers of value (they have to be to sustain any kind of longevity) but you can be the best Life Coach/Yoga Teacher/Financial Expert in the world and it doesn't mean anything if no one knows about you. To me there is nothing more painful, sadder and more maddening than unused, dormant talent. It makes me want to scream! And we are all guilty of letting our talents lie sleeping, but some of us much more than others. We know who we are.

Here are some techniques and tricks I learned throughout my 10 years in sales that I apply to many areas of my life.

1. **You gotta own what you have to offer.** Be clear, specific and assertive about what you are

good at. Focusing on your strengths will get you much further, much faster than worrying about your weaker areas.

2. **You have to explain it in a way that people understand.** Don't over complicate. Even the best doctors and scientists explain things in simple ways, for people of any age to interpret. Can you explain your hustle in just a sentence? You will lose your target market's attention if your message/offering is too complex.

3. **Give, a lot, before asking.** In publishing this is pretty much the law of getting started. In order to be paid to write you need to write a lot for free first, show some samples of your work and ideally have (even a very small) following. A personal blog completely counts! Most people slip up here. I hear them say things like, "Why would I put free instructional videos on YouTube? People should pay for those!" or "Why would I do a guest blog post on that person's blog? I don't want to give their blog any of my good material." This is completely the wrong approach.

4. **Invest in other people.** Your time, energy and in some cases, a little money. My biggest hobby is to read. I read a lot and therefore make a lot of recommendations. I have a trick that has worked really well for me for years. If I meet

someone I love or want to thank someone for their advice or simply feel called to give something (this happens often to me – remember, it's all about the giving!) I send them a book. It can be a digital book or physical book – both are great. You can gift a Kindle book via Amazon immediately if the recipient has a Kindle. People are so touched by books, especially ones that are useful to them. Try quantifying the price of a touching, helpful book – you can't! The returns are endless. Some are even less than $5. Plus – no one gives anyone anything for free so it's extra special. Try it! Also, be a connector. This is important. Connect people with opportunities and other people.

Over to you.

Think about where the people who might want to buy your product or service are online or offline. What do they read? Where do they hang? Brainstorm websites that you can pitch ideas to and see what their articles are about. If you are a health coach maybe you could pitch to Shape Magazine, "5 things you don't know about kale." If you are a career counselor maybe you could post on LinkedIn, "10 common resume mistakes." Where are your potential clients and what can you teach them in 500-800 words?

Lessons From A Leader: Fiona McKinnon, Founder, Turn Left Digital

Fiona is an experienced media consultant within the digital advertising industry. Her experience is global, having built businesses, launched products and mentored teams across the U.K., Europe, Australia and North America. Fiona founded Turn Left Digital at the end of 2014 and specializes in advising agencies, advertisers and ad tech businesses on technology innovation, operational efficiencies and cross Atlantic market launch strategies. Clients in her first year include CNN, SABMiller, Reuters and The Guardian.

Susie: What are the 3 biggest things that stop people from going out on their own?

Fiona: Fear, confidence and direction. I think most people would say that finances are the reason, which is part of fear, but I don't believe that money is the main blocker. By side hustling, you can minimize the financial fear and build your ideas at a pace that is comfortable for your situation.

Susie: What is your advice for attracting clients quickly?

Fiona: Be prepared to put yourself out there. These days that doesn't just have to be in the real world but can be through online and social relationships as well. Always be networking and looking for opportunities. Every conversation, and I mean *every* conversation can create business for you, whether it be an idea, a contact or an invaluable second opinion, all the way through to a contract or sale. Networking without research is only a half job however, so keep on top of trends, your competitors (who can also be partners) and general economic and market influences that can generate lead ideas or a shift in positioning. And follow up! I keep a list of people to speak to each week with no agenda other than to keep relationships strong. If you build genuine, strong relationships I believe that when the time is right, the opportunities will arise. My first year of business was driven by a mixture of friends of friends (old and new), Facebook, LinkedIn, contacts through charity work and free business network events. Finally, please, say thank you when someone does take the time out of their day to listen, advise, give you their business card or talk about your hustle. However small you may feel the gesture was at the time, it meant something to them as well – and you never know where chance meetings might lead.

Susie: What has been the biggest difference between running a business and working full-time as an employee?

Fiona: Freedom to be in control of my life, which means the ability to spend more time with friends and family, more time to travel and to do the things that make me happy. This doesn't necessarily mean that I work less, but the ability to be flexible with my time means my energy and focus is more suited to me. For example, I like working on projects on weekend afternoons, but I have Thursdays to myself during the week. On a practical level, I enjoy focusing on the job I have been asked to do with no internal meetings, staff training sessions or development plans to worry about.

Susie: What were your biggest fears when you started?

Fiona: That I wouldn't get any work; that I would fail in the minds of other people. I soon realized that worrying about what other people think is futile, and that I had to be doing this for me first and foremost.

Susie: What do you love most about running your own company?

Fiona: That it is all down to me. That can be scary, but it is also empowering. The freedom and energy of being in control of the decisions I make has led to other ideas forming, and I am now side hustling on my original side hustle! I also love the fact that I have inspired friends to think about working for themselves and following their passions.

Susie: What advice would you give to anyone wanting to start a side hustle?

Fiona: It is easy to say just go for it, but the time has to be right for you. Otherwise the fear, confidence and direction blockers I mentioned earlier will take over! Seek out others in the same stage of development – and beyond. Do your research, join online groups, don't underestimate the benefits of professional help. I have an accountant, financial advisor and coach/mentor that have all been instrumental in keeping me on track. But, it has to come from you, so really consider what your side hustle means to you. Then, every day do something to achieve that goal. I carry a notebook with me and I am constantly writing down strategies, ideas, contacts, names, products, plans. The ah-ha moment for the startup Turn Left came to me on a bus in India! My second project has been with me since I was 14 years old, but the time to bring it to life is right now. So, my advice is simple: Follow your dreams!

Chapter Ten:
The Why And The How Of Self Promotion

"You wouldn't worry so much about what others think of you if you realized how seldom they do."
~ Eleanor Roosevelt

"If being an egomaniac means I believe in what I do and in my art or music, then in that respect you can call me that... I believe in what I do, and I'll say it."
~ John Lennon

HERE'S the cold, hard truth. It's no one else's job to like you but you. How do you feel if your burning desire that wants to manifest as a killer side hustle remains silent? Do you like yourself? If you, in the words of Wayne Dyer, "die with your music still inside you," are you OK with yourself? I doubt that very much. Besides, other people are too concerned with their own stuff – their bills, their weight, their Facebook account, to judge your new entrepreneurial venture.

I was terrified when I put out my first video. These were the thoughts circling in my mind:

"WTF? Everyone is going to think I am so dumb/showy/full of myself!"

"Who actually cares about what I have to say?"

"Oh man, my frenemies are just gonna laugh their heads off."

"I look gross. It's too close up. I should have thought this through more."

"Once I post this it's for life. It's not safe."

Now I put out videos regularly and feel a twinge of both nerves and excitement when a new one comes out. The philosopher Goethe said, "Everything is hard before it is easy." Of course I hope people like them. But the process is no longer terrifying like it used to be and I am OK if some people don't like them.

One of the most common concerns people have when I coach them is putting the work they are doing "out there." I totally get it. When I was working full time I had this nagging feeling that I was waiting for my "real life" to begin. It, of course, already had. I had found my real life's work but was just so scared to talk about it.

I told my friends one by one about how I was training as a life coach, sharing with them the course that I was doing at NYU. Your friends will congratulate and support you. But my friends were not necessarily going to be my clients. I had to generate some. And there are no clients without awareness. You've got to put the word out about your work and promote yourself. You can be the best life coach/interior designer/stand-up comedian on the planet but it doesn't mean anything unless other people know about it.

I started a newsletter that I sent out on Sundays – and still do – to my entire contact list (with permission to unsubscribe of course). I shared some of my favorite quotes, insights that I had on various life topics and snippets/stories from the great books I was reading by Deepak Chopra, Jack Canfield, James Altucher, Tim Ferriss and Marianne Williamson. I've listed them at the back of this book.

I grew this list by emailing every single contact in my LinkedIn, Facebook and Twitter networks, asking if they would like to be added to my free weekly wellness newsletter. I had more than 3,000 contacts on LinkedIn alone that I had grown over my career in sales at the time and as a result my list grew to around 700 people within weeks. I also shared some of my own work on LinkedIn. This was a really subtle way of letting people know about the work I was doing – and by reading my content they got to know my coaching style.

I wanted to personalize each message I sent so that my offering came across as "less spammy". After all I did have a personal relationship with most of these people. At the time, LinkedIn wouldn't allow me to do the mail merge kind of message I was looking for, incorporating each persons first name and bulk emailing, so I hired a virtual assistant from Brickwork India to send out ~3,000 individual messages through my profile! It probably cost me a few hundred dollars and it took my assistant around 25 hours. The cost was well worth it as I could focus my attention on being paid to coach and it got things moving with my subscriber list. This turned out to be a great productivity hack. Lesson learned: don't try and be a hero by taking on absolutely every task in your business. Analyze the opportunity cost. What you are you really giving up by trying to "save money" taking on a task yourself? Time? Even more money?

Then, in every third newsletter or so I would share that I had coaching slots open and this drove a lot of referrals my way. I also changed my Twitter account and Facebook profile over time to reflect my life coaching work rather than my corporate job.

You may be proud to be a quiet achiever, but making peace with self-promotion matters.

Before you recoil at that expression, let me share a little secret. Shyness, being reserved, being cool – or whatever we default to as our reason for not self-promoting, does not necessarily equal humility. We don't wish to put ourselves on the line for criticism so we do nothing and mask it with an over-modest, "Oh I'm not a self-promoter."

Let me share with you why there is nothing brave or beneficial about that. If I have learned anything from my decade-long corporate sales career, it's that we are ALL in fact selling something, all the time. Every single one of us. Promotion is not reserved for smooth-talking realtors or those rocking retail careers. Teachers, H.R. professionals and dog-walkers are all unofficial sales people too. We all persuade and influence other people every day. In our resumes, in our self evaluation performance reviews at our job, in the way we dress, with our very selectively chosen, super considered social media posts, on our Tinder profiles, *everything* – we are all selling who we are and what we offer the world, constantly.

So why should we be afraid to promote something, a side hustle/business, that exists to impact the lives of others? We shouldn't.

Get used to the fact that it's the new normal. Do you flinch when you see someone sharing a recent job promotion online or an exciting development in their business? I doubt it. We expect to see these posts and when we like the person (and we almost always do if we are following them), we cheer them on. Other people will do the same for you. And if they don't? Well that's cool too. Leave them to it. I spent an hour talking to Kris Jenner when I interviewed her. She said to me: "It's sad that there are people somewhere, hiding behind their computer and writing cruel things about others on social networks. As my life has evolved and I have been on my own journey, I certainly feel vulnerable and beaten down at times but I know the importance of brushing myself off and getting back up." Whatever you think of her, she has created a billion dollar family empire.

Self-promotion means you will only want to put your best work out into the world, as you are accountable for it. It opens up opportunities too. When an online startup is looking for a consultant to lead a project, or newlyweds are seeking out an interior designer, who will be top of mind? The people they hear about who are doing great things! Don't let self-consciousness prevent you from progressing.

And as for what people think? James Altucher talks about the rule of thirds. One third of people will like you, one third of people won't like you and the other third won't care about you. Focus on the third that counts!

You may hear the term "content marketing" thrown around a lot. What is it? We have already touched on this, but it is producing and sharing valuable content, for free, with the intent to make a sale in the future – from how to style your hair with a beachy wave to how to whip up the perfect summer salad. Pure and simple. Consumers are spoiled for choice these days, so in order to appeal to them, earn their trust and have them buy from you, you need to add value to their lives and have them get to know you by what you share.

Whether it's through a weekly directing your audience to you blog posts, video tutorials, webinars, free samples of a product or a free introductory class, people want to "try before they buy". It's that straightforward. It builds familiarity and trust but it's also where most people slip up. That's why the average blogger gives up after their first post – they get frustrated about the fact that they aren't famous or making money after 5 minutes. But guess what? It, as with any business, takes time, consistency (and twenty blog posts) before anyone notices you.

The unfortunate thing here is that most people are unaware of how to allocate their time when it comes to producing vs. promoting. They aren't aware that as amazing as their content is, it's important that people get to SEE IT.

You are in this for the long game, my friend. And your self-approval is all that counts. Doing work that matters to you is your only real obligation to yourself and to the world. You have the opportunity right now, no matter how late it might feel, to live your life the way that is true to you.

I saw a great Instagram post once, that said, "First they will ask you why you are doing it, later they will ask you how you did it." I hear this a lot. People were shocked I was leaving such a good career. And now they say: "The C.E.O. of XYZ is paying you to advise them?! How do you even get that kind of work?" Or, "How did you get featured in X publication?" I chuckle to myself. When I was still working full time I hated being asked these questions in front of my boss. I used to say, "I'll put it in a book one day and you can read about it." And now you are.

Soon enough people will want to know how you created such a killer side hustle too!

Over to you.

Think of 1-3 people who support and believe in you, no matter what. Think of these people in moments of doubt or when putting the word "out there" about your work.

How can you connect with and add massive value to your audience periodically? What format/medium will you use to do this? What will the frequency be? The best content marketers go months without selling a single thing. It really solidifies the trust of their audience.

Chapter Eleven:
What You Don't Know About Failure

"This may come as a surprise to you but failure is an illusion. No one ever fails at anything. Everything you do produces a result. Failure is a judgment. It's just an opinion."
~Dr. Wayne Dyer, American Philosopher and Author

"Worry is a way to pretend that you have knowledge or control over what you don't – and it surprises me, even in myself, how much we prefer ugly scenarios to the pure unknown."
~Rebecca Solnit, Writer

"SUSIE, the General Manager would like to see you." My heart seized in my chest. "This is it!" I thought to myself. "I am getting promoted!" I was young, naïve, ambitious – and a little cocky – when I started out in my career. I joined my first company in an entry-level support role and I was desperate to get into sales. I spent all my time with the sales team, listening to them, helping them with their clients, upselling whenever I had the chance. "They have to be noticing this great work!" I kept thinking rather confidently to myself **while totally ignoring the data entry I was supposed to be doing.**

So when the big boss wanted to see me, I was ready. I dabbed on some lip-gloss and strutted up those stairs, prepared to gracefully accept my promotion. Oh, and I was gonna request business cards too (in my mind, business cards meant that I had hit the BIG time).

As soon as my butt hit the chair these words slapped me in the face, "Susie, we're letting you go. It's not working out."

Full body sting. Breathing stopped. Heart sank. Whaaaaat?!?!

And so I got fired in my early twenties. Rejection can simultaneously be the most awful blow and most awesome wake-up call (and course correct). It can feel like the biggest failure, especially when delivered – often very abruptly – when you're least expecting it. I once heard an interesting analogy about success and failure. They are actually on the exact same road – success is just farther down that road. And there is no such thing as the wrong path.

It's critical we cover failure here, as make no mistake, you will experience some setbacks in your side hustle that feel like failure. Here are some of my more recent ones:

- I neglected to include a simple link to my website from articles that were shared globally over 100,000 times (people couldn't find me easily: a massive lost opportunity). If you've spent any time working for an online business, you'll have a rough idea of how much potential business (through conversion) may have been lost here!

- When the time came for me to create one, I spent way too much on a website with an outdated theme that I had to replace shortly afterwards because it wasn't secure and couldn't be updated (pricey). You can create your own website via the free resources I have listed at the back. My clients have started profitable hustles with $0 and lots of heart!

- I wrote 70 percent of a book I decided I didn't like, so I didn't publish it. I realized that it sounded good to other people rather than felt good and authentic to me – oh the hours spent!

- I created my first online product and told my partners it would be ready in April. It was ready in October.

I have done too much at once. I have another partly completed course that I won't finish and multiple proposals that I won't send out simply because they are not the right thing for me right now. It has taken me a long time to realize less with deeper focus is better. And only your intuition can guide you on what is right! So listen. And focus on 1-2 things at a time, maximum, as you are starting out. Add more once you start to catch your stride. You are already working a job so focus is critical in your side hustle hours!

Sure I rue my wasted energy, hours and lost cash. But it was all part of the learning curve and hey, in business, sometimes you lose a little money. That is why I recommend getting paying clients before creating business cards or a professional website – or anything in fact. You don't need them to start.

Side note: This is another reason the side hustle is so awesome! You are already making money. You are in a better position to take a small financial hit if one happens.

"Ever tried, ever failed. No matter. Fail. Fail again. Fail better."
~Samuel Beckett

A rejection story I like to retell is in reference to a big online publication that I really, really wanted to write for. I approached the editor multiple times with no luck. About a month or two later, they randomly published some of my work, obviously through a syndication agreement they have with another publication I had written for.

This piece was shared many times and I had hundreds of new email subscribers as a result of this one republication. I thought to myself, "This is it! I'll approach the editor one more time and tell them that there is plenty more where that came from if they'd like me to write for

them!" I emailed the editor. DENIED. What can you do?!
Ha.

I love this passage from "The Success Principles" by
Jack Canfield:

Herbert True, a marketing specialist at Notre Dame
University, found that:

- *44 percent of salespeople quit trying to sell to a prospect*
  after the first call
- *24 percent quit after the second call*
- *14 percent quit after the third call*
- *12 percent quit trying to sell to their prospect after their*
  fourth call

This means that 94 percent of all sales people quit by the
fourth call. But 60 percent of all sales are made after the fourth call.
This revealing statistic shows that 94 percent of all sales people don't
give themselves a chance at 60 percent of the prospective buyers. You
might have the capacity, but you also have to have the tenacity! To be
successful you have to ask, ask, ask, ask, ask!

Amen, Jack.

Let me ask you this. What do you think that 94
percent would say if they were asked about their sales career?
They would probably say they failed. But did they? Hells no.
They just gave up too soon. In fact as a coach nothing
saddens me more than when a talented person gives up out
of hopelessness or feeling like a failure. You never know
how close the brink of a break could be. Woody Allen said
that, "80 percent of success is showing up." So show up!

Here is what you need to remind yourself of when
you experience rejection in your side hustle. You are not

alone. Anna Wintour was fired by Harper's Bazaar. "Everyone should be sacked at least once in their career because perfection doesn't exist," the Vogue editor-in-chief told Alastair Campbell in his new book, "Winners: And How They Succeed."

Oprah Winfrey was pulled off the air as an evening news reporter and was told that she was "unfit for TV." Michael Jordan was cut from his high school basketball team. Walt Disney was fired from a local newspaper when his editor told him he lacked imagination. Mark Cuban was fired from his job at a computer store – and that was the last day he ever worked for anyone else. Wahoo!

For me, getting fired made me realize what I am not suited to and made me assess what I am good at. My subsequent careers have been rewarding, fulfilling and awesome. I needed the wakeup call to get out of what was a completely unfitting job.

J.K. Rowling admits that "Harry Potter" was rejected by 12 publishing houses. Here is what she said about failure in her Harvard Commencement Speech in 2011:

"Failure in life is inevitable. It is impossible to live without failing at something, unless you live so cautiously that you might as well not have lived at all – in which case, you fail by default."

A lot of my readers write to me about this. You are afraid that you are not fulfilling your potential. You are scared that your life is wrong somehow. You feel as if you are betraying yourself and your calling every morning on your commute to work.

This is a note I received from someone who is part of my online community:

"I recently moved to the U.S.A. with the hopes that I would have more opportunity and possibility to figure out what it is that I really want to do in life professionally. I have many interests and the thought of choosing any single one makes me a little sad because I feel like I would be neglecting all the others. Currently working in a corporate setting while I try to explore during evenings and weekends. :)"

Your side hustle is the most practical, possible and awesome opportunity to pursue your passions. You can follow them and really build something big from them. The failure is not getting started. The failure is when you do nothing and, as J.K. Rowling says, you fail "by default." Inaction is action. Believe this and let it steer you towards harnessing your dormant talents and greatness. And in doing so you are going to have to do something really important: let go (or rapidly reduce the influence of) what other people think.

I never would have met my completely compatible husband unless I had the bad experience of my first marriage. Unless I got fired from my first job I would never have gotten started as a recruiter which kicked off my decade long successful sales career. Unless I truly hated my last boss I would not have had the courage to quit my corporate job and commit to working as a coach, writer and consultant. Find the good in the failure. It's always there.

Over to you.

Think of a recent personal or professional failure. How can you use this experience as an opportunity to learn something about yourself?

Lessons From A Leader: Derek Flanzraich, Founder & C.E.O., Greatist

Derek is an entrepreneur on a mission to help the world think about health – with a healthy attitude. He is the founder and C.E.O. of Greatist, a next-generation media startup working to build the first truly trusted, consumer-facing health brand for millennials. Greatist is currently the fastest-growing media site in the digital health space, with almost 10 million unique visitors per month.

Susie: What was it that inspired you to take an entrepreneurial route over a conventional employee/corporate route?

Derek: After graduating from college I decided I wanted to start my own thing. It sort of clicked with me that whatever I was going to start, it had to be my life's mission, my passion. The minute I realized that, I realized that I may as well start now. That really propelled me to start my own thing and five years later I'm glad I did.

Susie: How would you describe your passion or mission? Can you define that in a sentence or two?

Derek: I grew up one of the biggest kids in the class, struggling with my weight and really feeling like everything I turned to, every T.V. show I turned on, every Google search that I did, every magazine that I opened, was making me feel worse instead of better. I was stunned that there really wasn't a brand that was empowering and focused on not what people were eating but why. Not what people were doing to workout, but why they wanted to workout in the first place. That's why I started Greatist. I think Greatist's mission is really my personal mission too, which is to help the world think of health in this different way and give the world a healthy attitude.

Susie: How did you overcome the fear of failure?

Derek: I'm not sure I ever did. I still feel those things. I just don't let it stop me. I let it fuel me and I see this as a big journey of learning. I'm confident. I'm hell-bent on building and making this difference that I want to make in the world. I won't allow anything to get in my way.

Susie: What is it that keeps you going in moments of exhaustion or fatigue?

Derek: Breathing and meditation is important. My real secret is that I care so much about Greatist and I want us to succeed so badly. But I don't want to kid anyone. It's definitely the hardest thing I've ever done. There have been times when it's just been unbelievably hard. I do think that if the reason you're doing it is for something bigger than you, then you keep going.

Susie: As a leader, what's your take on making mistakes?

Derek: I learn almost entirely by fucking things up first – and sometimes I have to fuck it up a couple times. I wish that wasn't true, but it's super true for me at least. I think success is really not about not making mistakes, but about (and this isn't my phrase) mistakes well-handled.

Susie: What would you say is the best thing about entrepreneurial life so far?

Derek: You can create the thing that you most want to see in the world. Greatist didn't exist a few years ago, and now it's a thing and 10 million people engage with it on a regular basis. Literally on a monthly basis, millions and millions and millions of people are reading the kind of thing I wished existed.

Susie: What has been the best piece of business advice you've received?

Derek: In the early days people told me over and over again that I shouldn't be ashamed or embarrassed to ask for help – but I was. I considered it a weakness. As I continue my journey I realize how powerful asking for help can be, because I always needed a lot of help, but I felt like my job was not to ask for it; to pretend I knew the answers. The real truth is I know less of the answers than I ever thought, but in asking for help, you unlock the opportunity to receive help.

Susie: Do you still ask for help?
    Derek: Oh my God, all the time.

Susie: How do you define success?
    Derek: Building Greatist.

Chapter Twelve:
How To Leverage Your Talent To Make Money

"What's easy to you is amazing to others."
~ Derek Sivers, Writer and Entrepreneur

"The best way to do it is to do it."
~ Amelia Earhart

WHEN most of us think about our passion we rarely think of it making us money. It's true that not everything you are passionate about should be a revenue source. What separates a hustle from a hobby is money. Pure and simple. If you are an incredible cook you might want to reserve your talents for people you love. You don't have to want to cook for others or teach others your culinary secrets. But if you do – think of how many people would love to learn how to cook, or the entire market out there that might enjoy your gastronomic creations. Martha Stewart started out as a local caterer. Bethenny Frankel baked and delivered her own cakes: Bethenny Bakes. You need to identify which passion you would like to make a business – one that can live and breathe and sustain and one that you won't resent as it grows and demands more of your creativity, time and energy. Then – to business!

The secret to success is being resourceful. The number one way to do this is to use your network. It's bigger than you think. Don't be afraid to let your contacts know that you're open for business by posting your side hustle work on social media and starting an email list updating people with your offers. Most people will support you. After some time my corporate clients became some of my biggest supporters and even coaching clients (turns out a few had, or wanted to begin their own hustles).

To reinforce my point: So many of my coaching and consulting clients spend more time worrying about their website and business cards when they start out than they do about getting paying clients – I started making thousands in extra monthly income BEFORE I had a website or a business card.

I also could have procrastinated for years before writing this book – waiting for this interview or that interview. I won't lie – I was slow in publishing this (6 months behind schedule). But I pushed it out.

Here was the email I sent to my friends when I was looking for coaching clients. You can use this as the basis for your reach out!

Hello friends!

Please forgive the mass email.

For those of you who do not know, I am currently attending New York University to get a certificate in Personal Coaching. I am now ready to take on some new clients (at a very affordable rate) for experience as I gain my certification. It is preferable for me to coach people I do not know, so I am asking for your help in finding someone you might know who would be willing to engage in this exciting process with me. It is a 6-week engagement for an hour a week (on phone or in person). I am enthusiastic to work with people who are committed to drive positive change in their life.

I need to call any referrals by 11/18 for a 15-minute call to see if there's a good fit. If you could send me names/phone #'s of anyone that might be interested, please let me know as soon as possible.

Also, many of you already expressed interest in wanting to be coached as well. If so, please send me your most suitable contact information, as there might be classmates of mine that I can refer you to.

I am very passionate about this field and know it can be extremely rewarding for anyone!

Look forward to hearing from you.

Thanks so much – Susie

Start where you are with what you have. The trick to kicking off a successful side hustle in record time is to put word out – get orders or service requests and just BEGIN. It's a common misconception that you need a lot of money to start a business. Several people have said things to me along the lines of "Well you had all of this money saved from a lucrative career, so it must have been easy for you to invest it into your business", but my initial set up costs were precisely $0. In fact, I made it a condition of my side hustle that it had to pay for itself, so I had paying clients before I spent a cent on my business. I knew that if my side hustle were not self-sustaining, I'd never be able to grow it to a point that would allow me to quit my job without dipping into my savings.

You don't need an office or studio. You can help someone with their resume over Skype or in a café, for example. You can show people how to house train their puppies in their apartment and in the park. You can be a freelance web designer and work from anywhere remotely.

My friend Amber, a photographer and videographer, generates up to $4K a month for just the price of a latte or sandwich with a new client (see her interview at the back)!

Look around you. Who can you add to your email list? How can you grow this list? What did you leave untapped? Your volleyball group? Old co-workers? College alumni? The parents of your children's friends? What Facebook and LinkedIn groups are you in? Can your spouse help with his or her friends? Remember – the world needs your product or service so you must not be bashful in sharing it!

While social media is great for building brand awareness, it's very noisy and can become quite expensive. The changing nature of the various algorithms each platform uses and ever shifting user sentiment has meant that it's become increasingly challenging (and *more* expensive) to compete with already fully established influencers and brands.

I get it, having a big social media following is sexy, however, many U.S. marketing executives believe that email marketing contributes as much to their revenue as banner ads, their website and all of their social media avenues combined! This is why building and nurturing a list is so critical. Regardless of what happens in the social media ecosystem, you have an incredibly effective way of communicating with your audience. This doesn't mean you should abandon all social media efforts, it just means that email marketing is still an incredibly powerful tool for your side hustle.

Here are just a few things you can do to build your list, social media presence and brand:

- Extend an invitation to those already in your network (social media, personal email directory). Side note: always ask permission before adding people to your list, unless they sign up themselves.

- Be a guest presenter/blogger for another business, show, website or blog and add a link for people to sign up to your site/newsletter. Most publications are totally fine with this unless there is a conflict of interest in your offering.

- Include a very apparent sign up or opt in page on your site. You will be surprised how even then many people who visit your site and love it will not sign up, so make it very visible.

- Create an "opt-in gift". Some people cringe when they hear this but it is a fair trade. Someone gives you their email address and you give them something of value up front. Pay attention the next time you visit a website – they almost always want your email address and will often give you something in exchange. E.g. a report on the latest stock trends or a free introductory video training to Krav Maga.

- Nurture your list and potential sign-ups. Assume that anyone on your list could be a potential client, business partner or referral. Add incredible and consistent value via weekly or monthly emails before asking for anything in return. Again, most people struggle with this.

It may be hard to see, but even non-web based businesses can benefit from building an online following. Using a hairdresser as an example, you may send out a monthly video tutorial or post your work regularly on Instagram, showing the latest hair trends or, "How to do a messy bun for a casual date." Adding this kind of value first leads to people saying, "Hey, I really like him/her, I want to get to their studio/salon/class." It gets people comfortable and familiar with you being an authority on the subject and, over time, increases demand to hire you.

Side note: My friend Hannah is editing this book. She was a friend of a friend and as I began writing she helped me out here and there with great advice – how to work with PR teams to schedule a celebrity interview, how to have a killer opening line... She's a pro. We met at a picnic in Central Park and became friends over our joint love of reading and writing. She is an excellent freelance editor/writer and her current side hustle is helping me put this together! One time she even hired me as a life coach to run a vision board event for The Newswomen's Club of New York. We have hired each other in the past couple of years. What does this tell you? People are everywhere. Get to know them. Always be cultivating your network!

An Important Note About Imposter Syndrome

Here is one thing you need to know: Imposter Syndrome is the main culprit preventing anyone starting and making money from a side hustle (or any entrepreneurial venture). Be aware of this sneaky, ever-present syndrome. Imposter syndrome is what we experience when we feel we don't deserve our accomplishments or are in any position to start a business. When we experience success we feel we've fooled others into thinking we are capable and attribute our achievements to blind luck or good timing. Our inability to accept our gifts means we feel like a fraud or an imposter – maybe even waiting to be exposed. This is why so many potentially beautiful side hustles never launch. We say, "Who am I to…"

Most common in high-achieving women, imposter syndrome not only prevents us from enjoying success, it also massively limits our current potential. Feeling non-deserving and like a fake, we turn down wonderful new opportunities and creative ideas. Imposter syndrome is the killer of many "what-might-have-beens."

Does that sound like you? It sure sounds a lot like the excuses I hear all the time (including from myself on my bad days). People I coach always tell me they are "not ready" for the next step. Moving cities. Starting an entrepreneurial venture. Online dating. Applying for a role at a prestigious company. The truth is, we're never ready. But those who get what they want in this world proceed anyway. In the words of Susan Jeffers, they "feel the fear and do it anyway." They know there is nothing to lose and a whole lot to gain by taking action. And the more you do it, the easier it becomes over time. It can also feel quite thrilling. I have never felt more alive than when I have moved countries, quit jobs, and launched entrepreneurial projects.

<u>The Kick-Ass Truth About Multiple Revenue Streams</u>

One thing I tell many of my clients when it comes to starting their side hustle is to be conscious of having multiple revenue streams, particularly in the beginning. The same way your hustle is a nice hedge against income uncertainty with your job, having multiple streams of income is also a hedge against the business cycle and changes in your client's demands. **Remember this too, always.** You never do your best work when you are desperate for cash. You are too stressed out. The more income flowing your way the more creative you can be and selective in terms of opportunity. That's a big reason the side hustle is so magical.

As your business grows, having multiple revenue streams will also allow you to determine what areas you would like to focus on (from an enjoyment perspective) and what areas you should focus on (business perspective) and expand/contract accordingly.

Some income streams may even be passive, such as selling a product, eBook or course online, rental income from that property portfolio you have slowly started building. Or even being a referral source for others (and taking a commission from successful introductions like recruiters do). Here are just some of the ways my business makes money (in no particular order):

1. My blog via Google ads
2. 1:1 life coaching
3. Group coaching
4. Writing for large publications

5. Being a referral partner for other businesses and coaches
6. Executive coaching, consulting and advisory to startups
7. Selling online courses, The Ultimate Side Hustle Starter Guide and How to Get A Raise in 30 Days.
8. This book!
9. Being a spokesperson on the topic of confidence for large companies
10. Hosting events such as vision board parties

There is a caveat here. While I was a full-time employee, I really only focused on #2 and #4 to avoid burnout. I added all additional sources of income thereafter.

Over to you.

Collaborate with other hustlers and entrepreneurs at every opportunity. Find your tribe. The bigger your community the more "luck" you will have. Who do you know that already does some similar work in the field you want to enter? Brainstorm a list and reach out by adding value to these people!

Lessons From A Leader: Ellie Burrows, Founder & C.E.O., MNDFL

Ellie is the C.E.O. of MNDFL, New York City's premier meditation studio, as well as a certified personal development coach and writer. MNDFL enables people to feel good by offering traditional meditation techniques in an accessible manner. Ellie served as an executive in the film business, focusing on the business side of film: producing, selling, financing and attracting talent. When her meetings began to evolve into coaching sessions around effective communication and interpersonal relationships, she chose to pursue mindfulness and spirituality in a more meaningful way.

Susie: A lot of people have an idea to start a business but they rarely follow through. What made you the exception?

Ellie: I think the trick was that we never got ahead of ourselves. As meditators, we were able to be more present and in the moment. It was truly one tiny foot in front of the other when building MNDFL.

Susie: If someone has an idea for a business, whatever it may be, and they won't pursue it because they have a fear of failure and rejection, what advice would you give them?

Ellie: I would advise them to work on themselves before trying to work on a business. Human beings are very tribal and it does really take a village to do certain things. Getting help outside of yourself, whether that's in the form of a meditation teacher, therapist, spiritual advisor, life coach, or friend can be very beneficial. I highly recommend using outside sources to help you understand your own limitations so you can work with them rather than have them work against you.

Susie: I think asking for help or asking in general is really underestimated. What would you say to people who maybe feel a little shy to ask?

Ellie: People are shy to ask because they feel shame that they don't know something or think they're an imposition. This business exists because I asked a million questions.

Susie: What is the best thing so far about running a business?

Ellie: The deep satisfaction that comes along with knowing that you created something from nothing.

Susie: People who are reading this have (or want to have) a side hustle. Many of them want to transition from day jobs, they want to create big, beautiful things but struggle with impostor syndrome.

Ellie: I think everyone feels like a fraud at some point – it's unfortunately a function of the ego. We can be overly judgmental of ourselves or fearful that someone else is judging us too. I definitely still have moments where I think it's wild that I run a business. I sometimes catch myself thinking, "I do not feel old enough to be in charge of this." or "C.E.O.? Is this a costume I'm wearing?!?" When I catch myself doing that, I'll gently remind myself that those thoughts are simply thoughts and then I practice letting go of them.

Susie: What has been the coolest part of having a business?

Ellie: The human-to-human interaction, especially when someone is *so pleased* with what we've created.

Susie: Because you created it?

Ellie: The gratitude that gets exchanged, their gratitude that we created this space, my gratitude that they're here and sitting in the studio, that whole thing is just a crazy, amazing feeling. That's probably the best part.

Susie: Because you built and own something that generates joy in other people?

Ellie: Yes, their joy generates joy in me.

Susie: How do you respond to the different types of feedback you get?

Ellie: Feedback is enormously helpful, both the good and bad kind. It's essential to the businesses growth. When you start your own business I think you need to know that not everything you're making is going to appeal to absolutely every person on the planet. If one person doesn't like it, you can't go into a state of devastation because the truth is there are billions of humans on this planet and it's not going to be for everybody. Not everyone is going to like your business and that's okay, but it shouldn't discourage you from doing it.

Chapter Thirteen:
Why You Must Start Your Side Hustle – The Spiritual Reason

"It is better to live your own destiny imperfectly than to live an imitation of somebody else's life with perfection."
~ *The Bhagavad Gita*

"Let the world know why you're here and do it with passion... Don't die with your music still inside you."
~ *Dr. Wayne Dyer, American Philosopher and Author*

"Remember that wherever your heart is, there you will find your treasure."
~Paulo Coelho, The Alchemist

WHAT does your life look like when you stand back and see the big picture? Or picture your 80-year-old self lying in bed, considering the life you've had and all the choices you've made? The ancient Greeks used to "practice death every day." They would foster perspective on their life daily and allow this to infuse all of their thoughts, actions and behavior. In "Regrets of The Dying," Bronnie Ware, a hospice nurse, writes about how many of the patients she nursed in their final days regretted that they lived a life other people expected of them and not the life they truly wanted to live. When we use our talents, skills and gifts, we don't leave room for regret. We all secretly know this. What bigger motivation can there be to pursue work that you really love?

Of all the people I coach, their finest hour is when, in the words of the incredible author James Altucher, they decide to "choose themselves." Choosing yourself means doing work that you love on your terms. Not work that is tasked to you by a boss or expected from you by any figure of authority. When you step out of a structure that tells you what you do, you are in a position to choose what you want to do. This is what your free hours are for!

You choose. It's all you.

When you see the whole picture of your life it allows you to have a lot more perspective in your decision-making. Steve Jobs said something in his commencement speech at Stanford University in 2005, which still gives me chills every time I hear it:

"Remembering that I'll be dead soon is the most important tool I've ever encountered to help me make the big choices in life. Almost everything — all external expectations, all pride, all fear of

embarrassment or failure – these things just fall away in the face of death, leaving only what is truly important. Remembering that you are going to die is the best way I know to avoid the trap of thinking you have something to lose. You are already naked. There is no reason not to follow your heart."

If there is an impact that you know you want to make on the world, that tugs on your heart, I think we can all agree it makes complete sense to start your side hustle.

In fact, I would pay someone if they could change my mind about this. I also, not even consciously, made a decision in early 2016 to focus more on coaching people who are launching or building a business, whether it is a side hustle or full-time operation. Not only is this where I can provide the most help and encouragement, it's where I feel the most inspired and alive.

One of my first coaching clients said to me, "Susie, when I'm at work at an ad agency, all I do (secretly) is pin fashion looks together and research vintage jewelry." Her passion was so obvious – she created lookbooks on the weekends, followed designers on Instagram, and always looked beautifully downtown chic on a pretty tight budget – she just needed to step back to realize it. And now, two years later? She works nights and weekends as a personal stylist and plans to transition full-time.

Again – what is the worst that can happen? She won't like it. Clients will run dry. She will miss her old office environment and hate all the back end work that a business entails (accounting, taxes, website management). So what? She will get another job just like her last one (that might even pay more).

And... what is the best that can happen? She becomes a successful C.E.O. doing work she is completely obsessed with. She writes a book on style. She becomes best friends with top trendsetters; designers follow her on Twitter. She moves to Paris. She has celebrity clients and spends the winters in L.A. She launches her jewelry line. Who knows? The possibilities are endless. "I dwell in possibility," Emily Dickinson wrote. Well, so does my client. But she'd never know it unless she'd begun.

Over to you.

Write a letter from your 80-year-old self. Start, "Dear Me, I am so happy that in my life I wasn't afraid. I am so thankful that I..."

Write down all the things you secretly want to do. Don't hold back. Allow everything to just come up for you. This can go beyond your work and the impact that you make with it. But I know pursuing work that you love will be up there.

Lessons From A Leader: Stephanie St.Claire, Personal Consultant and Author

Stephanie St.Claire is NYC-based personal consultant who works with people to strategize a survival plan through setback, loss, and worst-case scenarios. Author of "11 Things I Wish I Knew When I Started My Business," she shares her philosophies and advice through her writing, workshops, and 1:1 session work.

Susie: You had a successful career in PR. What made you transition into entrepreneurship?

Stephanie: I had started in an assistant position in PR at the age of 40 and I was never going to hit the income I needed to build a robust financial future. When you start your own business, you start from ZERO – but I knew the potential to make money was totally correlated with my own hustle game, and I was ready to hustle. Let me be clear: I did NOT have a lot of confidence in my skill set as an entrepreneur... I had never run a full-scale business before. But I had the quixotic belief that if I took all the energy, enthusiasm, and work ethic I was using to build someone else's business and put that toward my own, I would be rewarded with all the profit.

Susie: You wrote a beautiful advice-based piece for your blog that was shared over 1 million times. What advice would you give to someone looking to become an entrepreneur in the coaching/writing space?

Stephanie: Give yourself two years to become fully financially self-sustaining. The first year is going to be all about you building a ground swell of clients and customers that trust you, remember you, and are slightly obsessed with you. You will do this by serving them in multiple ways through your writing, videos, free content you share with them on social, and through the letters you write to their inboxes. You almost have to untether yourself from the money and just keep giving. This drives everyone mad! They think they're doing something wrong or they have "cheap" customers that don't want to buy their offerings. But all that is happening is that you are building trust and nurturing relationships. The scales tip at some point – and you have

NO CONTROL over the timing of this, so please just surrender to that part. But one day you'll notice that you're working a lot less feverishly and the money you are making is double or triple what you were making in the early days. It's worth it!

Susie: What have been some of the biggest surprises along this entrepreneurial path?

Stephanie: I've been surprised by my own tenacity! Entrepreneurship is one of those things that mentally and emotionally expands you like parenthood or marriage... you aren't prepared for the different twists and turns in the road. But if you take each one as it comes, with patience and kindness toward yourself, you WILL grow to be the most tenacious person you know.

Susie: What first piece of advice would you go back and give yourself at the start of launching your business?

Stephanie: That running the business end is the first priority, not consulting or writing. You will spend 15 percent of the time doing what you love (your gift – in my case coaching and writing) and 85 percent of the time marketing, administrating, selling, strategizing your business, and answering a load of email. Survival will totally hinge on how quickly you adopt this role of Business Owner first, creator of pretty things, second. I would also have hired an assistant before year 5!

Susie: What keeps you going in moments of fear/doubt/stress?

Stephanie: I know that if I keep returning to the basics: self-care, structure, and the aim to simply serve others through my work, everything will be okay. I also know deep in my bones that I don't want to be doing anything else with my time and energy. I want to work on my own mission, not another company's. If I've lost my sense of humor about things, that's the danger sign I'm running toward burnout or I'm over analyzing. I'll usually step away from my desk for a few hours when that happens and get my center back.

Chapter Fourteen:
Why You Must Start Your Side Hustle – The Practical Reason

"Do what you have to do until you can do what you want to do."
~ Oprah Winfrey

"Why not me?"
~ Mindy Kaling

"Unused creativity is not benign. It metastasizes. It turns into grief, rage, judgment, sorrow, shame. We are creative beings. We are by nature creative. It gets lost along the way. It gets shamed out of us."
~ Brené Brown, "The Gifts of Imperfection"

OK, so let's get practical. Hopefully we feel pretty convinced that given our mortality, and the tremendous untapped talent and creativity we know we have lurking within us, we have to satisfy the inner stirring we are feeling. We need to seize it and nurture it and see what can happen. It's unhealthy not to. So why is the side hustle also practical?

Here are some key reasons:

1. You hedge against an uncertain economy – there is no such thing as job security anymore

2. You earn more money – so yes, you can feel good about your daily $4 latte, pay off some debt or go on that holiday

3. You learn new skills that are critical in this era – for example, sales, marketing, negotiation, networking, Wordpress, some form of CRM system, basic accounting and taxation. Skills that may benefit you in your day job too, until you no longer need it!

4. Set-up costs can be totally minimal – I started life coaching with no website, business cards or office. I charged $100 per hour, met people through my own network (LinkedIn, Facebook) and met clients in coffee shops or over Skype. I also managed to convince my company to cover the costs of my coaching studies. If you speak

up and ask you can uncover budgets you didn't
know existed!

5. You can totally work it around your schedule –
    nights and weekends are all yours to use plus
    the hours you can use are immense when you
    realize that capacity is a state of mind

6. Online resources leave you no excuses – you
    can contribute as a freelancer for 99designs,
    Fiverr (I was just reading about a woman who
    makes $9,000 a month – initially a side gig –
    doing voiceovers), Elance and Freelancer.com,
    which offer gigs from website bio writing to
    book cover design and language translation

7. You save money. Think about it. Time you
    spend building your business is time you are not
    at the bar, at the sample sale, at the 4-hour
    lunch or online shopping for ballet flats or golf
    clubs

8. You can tell your boss you're outta there one
    day because your side hustle dough matches (or
    exceeds) your salary

9. You might invent/write/build the next greatest
    thing that people need

10. The opportunities are truly unlimited unlike your (probably) limiting career. No glass ceilings or salary caps here!

If you're still not convinced, be aware that Sara Blakely created Spanx while selling fax machines full-time (and only when Spanx became one of Oprah's favorite things did she resign from her job). Khaled Hosseini wrote the best-selling book "The Kite Runner" while working full time in a hospital. Michael Burry pursued his hobby of financial investing in between shifts at Stanford Hospital as he finished his residency. He left medicine shortly after to pursue his side hustle full time, starting a hugely successful hedge fund, making hundreds of millions of dollars by correctly calling the sub prime mortgage crisis – he was the star of Michael Lewis' book "The Big Short" and portrayed by Christian Bale in the movie of the same name.

Elizabeth Gilbert, author of "Eat Pray Love," is a big mentor of mine (although she doesn't know it). In an interview with Cosmopolitan she said:

I am 46 now, and I look back at the people who I was hanging out with in my 20s, and there were some who had what looked to me at the time like infinite power and infinite promise and infinite possibility. And they never did anything with it. And then there were other people who I kind of dismissed and thought didn't have anything – and then those people just blew my mind with what they ended up creating. To me, the most boring question in the world is, "Who has talent?" and, "Who doesn't have talent?" Because I have seen that that is not really where it's at. We will never know. There is no objective measure that we could use to tell who is talented and who isn't talented.

You can only tell by what they make and what they make of their lives. I don't know how much natural talent I have. I know that I work harder than anybody I know... In my 20s... I was a bartender, I was a waitress, and I worked in a bookstore.

And you know, my first two books were written when I had three jobs. So sometimes when I hear people say, "I would love to do this but I don't have time!" Or, "Well, I have a real job and I would have to quit my job to write a book." And I'm like, you don't have to quit your fucking job to write a book.

In late 2015, I had brunch with two young women who have the same career that I used to have – they are sales directors in the online advertising sector. Both are brilliant and successful. One of them shared with me an idea that she has about launching an event planning business specific to a particular industry. The idea sounded great. But let me let you in on a little secret. Ideas are overrated. A good-enough idea executed upon is better than a tremendous idea only talked about over waffles and mimosas.

As soon as she shared it she started poking holes in it, "well I want to move out of New York one day so it won't be sustainable" and "I don't really have any experience in the hospitality sector." Ah, here you are again, our old friend fear. I wanted to scream – are you kidding me? You are a sales woman! You make shit happen and close against all odds in one of the most competitive spaces of all time!

I know that in her day job she contacted a client upwards of 20 times in order to secure just one 30 minute meeting. You think this young woman could not get a few venues to talk to her and pitch her ideas the same way she does every working day of her life? And doesn't every city in the country have some kind of event, every day? And so I asked (and you must ask yourself this too when your doubts creep in):

"Well, how might it work if I believed that it could?"

"What skills do I have that would work in my favor here?"

"How could it succeed in a way I have not necessarily thought of?"

And with those 3 questions this talented young woman solved her own problem. She said, "Shit, I am a sales person. I know how to persuade people. I know how to pitch ideas. I would just do my research [ding, ding, ding!] and tailor it to a new market."

Fait accompli, my friends.

Taking responsibility for your work and your hours on earth brings a lot of confidence into your life. It astounds me how many people feel their corporate skills – or any experience they have from years of working – are not transferable to a side business. Or they have not spent a single second making the logical connection that a lot of what they know is valuable can be used in other valuable ways, too.

If you haven't already read "The Alchemist" I beseech you to do so – look out for the expressions 'the language of the world' and 'all things are one.' There are no isolated or solitary life skills or experiences we go through that do not help us in our future experiences. Even the boring parts of our jobs (for me it was data entry and tracking revenue in an Excel spreadsheet) are now helpful in my business. It's all intertwined. Also, look at the back of this book for all my other resources that helped me launch my business, gave me killer advice and keep me going in times I lose motivation.

What do you have to lose? You are keeping your day job. Your rent continues to be paid. Your day job continues to support you in the same way it always has. You still have health insurance. But sorry, re-runs of "Homeland" won't support you. You have work to do. So let's get started. Are you with me?

Over to you.

Again, ask yourself these questions about your hustle idea:

"Well, how might it work if I believed that it could?"

"What skills do I have that would work in my favor here?"

"How could it succeed in a way I have not necessarily thought of?"

Chapter Fifteen:
The Beginning

HERE is a little universal truth that not everyone is aware of. When you walk in the direction of your dreams, take action, get busy and gain momentum, the universe greets you half way. Steven Pressfield in his book "Do The Work" calls this "assistance." It is very, very real.

In June 2012, I was feeling a little bored and uncomfortable at work but had not yet started side hustling. I wasn't really aware that you could, was not sure how to begin or what I would do. I was also afraid that my boss would get upset if my focus was not 100 percent on selling advertising technology. (You'll be happy to hear that this is increasingly untrue. Unless you are under a strict contractual obligation many employers actually support creative pursuits outside of work.)

One of the co-founders of the startup I worked for called me out of the blue about an opportunity. He asked if I was interested in working in D.C. for the remainder of the year to see if I could generate some political advertising revenue. To this day I am not sure why he asked me but I like to think that he saw me as someone who got results and was open to new projects.

This was unlike anything I had ever done before. I had absolutely no understanding of the U.S. political system. Nada. Zip. Zero. All I knew at that point was that Obama was running again – I was not even sure whom the Republican rival was (ha)! So not only did I give myself a crash course in U.S. politics, I watched CNN like an addict and read Politico like it was going out of style.

Then, between June and November, I spent the majority of my time in Washington D.C. selling video campaigns to political activation committees and advertising agencies. My new title was Political Sales Director and my second home became the W Hotel opposite The White House. Taxi drivers in D.C. recognized me. "Back to the W?" one asked while I was rushing in to his car on my phone with my high heels and small suitcase, taken aback that he knew my destination.

I worked that unique, difficult-to-penetrate and highly complex market like my life depended on it. One night I even had two steak dinners back to back – one at 6.30 p.m. and another at 9p.m. – to accommodate two different client schedules.

My guy said he would have been "thrilled" if I generated $500K in advertising dollars. By November 3rd, 2012, when the last voting polls closed on the west coast, I had generated almost $3 million. What is the moral of this story? I should carve my niche as a political expert? No. I had found my calling in Washington? Certainly not. The moral is this: you don't need whatever people think or tell you you need to achieve something awesome.

I had no political background. I wasn't even a U.S. citizen who could vote. This was my first time selling media campaigns. I had no reason to succeed apart from a belief that I could and an unwavering work ethic. As Mindy Kaling likes to say, "Why not me?"

Making that experience rock (and earning a sweet little bonus from it which I learnt to negotiate as my success grew – another lesson learned, *always* be asking for more), also showed me what I can do in a short amount of time with massive application and belief. And get this. The biggest deal I closed – around $800K or so – came from an off-chance tip from a new connection I had made.

I had a last-minute meeting on my way back to New York with a small firm I had not heard of before and almost couldn't make it work. But I felt called to go. This was not one of the meetings I had slaved to secure. It was a little universal wink and blessing – a reward for my hard work and dedication. When you get busy, the universe – always unpredictably but with more fervor than you can imagine – meets you half way and over-delivers. I have heard endless stories like this. This I know for sure. So often we don't give the universe the opportunity. We give up too soon or we don't even begin.

When this massive deal closed my boss bought champagne for the whole New York office and emailed a photo of me opening the bottle to the entire company. It was pretty freakin' awesome. I felt like a rock star. That year I won one of the 5 company awards they gave out at the holiday party for the entire global team in San Francisco (the irony was I was in Turks and Caicos with my husband and could not even accept it). I felt like one of those ballers who could not accept their VMA as they are on a shoot or doing something cool in a remote part of the world. Hey, a girl can dream, right?

Another time the universe rocked for my husband and me when we really needed it. Heath is the reason we live in the U.S. His hard work not only landed us in New York (his company transferred him here when he was 23), he negotiated (and landed) Green Cards for us. Anyone who has gone through the Green Card process knows it is a very long and arduous one. Without a Green Card, you are tied to the firm that you work for and many companies will not entertain visa sponsorship, which makes moving around difficult. Also, if you lose your job, you have to leave the country.

We love living in the U.S. more than anything else. So Heath (with massive universal assistance) secured our Green Cards via his firm. After seven years at one company he was ready to find a new role better suited to his long-term goals. He had really stuck it out for us over the years and embarking on a job search in a really competitive market felt overwhelming. Also, after seven years with an Australian company, with an Australian work culture it's natural to feel a bit anxious about changing to work for a big American company. But, the universe helped out once again.

I was on a business trip in Miami. The trip was rescheduled twice because of my client's schedule and we ended up at the Viceroy. (We almost stayed at a different hotel – there are plenty of variables at work here, which is why you just have to trust the universe!) Heath decided to join me and stay for the weekend.

We chose to have dinner at the hotel and, as I was ready before him, I headed down to the bar to grab a martini. I sat down just as the man next to me was presented with his meal, which looked delicious. I asked him what he ordered (seafood) and we got talking about the menu. When Heath arrived we were chatting about Miami, things to do there (the man was visiting for work too), plus a little bit about our backgrounds – the usual stranger small talk. Only it turns out the man was a Managing Director and business head at one of the companies Heath had really wanted to work for. Two weeks later, he was hired. Talk about a slam-dunk! Wow.

Think about it – the date, the hotel, the timing at the bar, the open seat, the seafood: everything conspired to make this happen for my husband. Luck? I don't think so. There is always a greater power at work than we can see or understand. Eighteen months later Heath loves his job and team.

Here is my final story about the universe being on your side. I quit my job in December 2014. It was a big and scary decision but after almost 18 months of side hustling (and averaging around $4,000 a month doing it) I was tired. I didn't have a good rhythm with my boss. We'd just moved into a new apartment and something told me I would be safe if I took the leap to work for myself full time in this new setting. It was terrifying but something inside me felt like I didn't really have a choice. I felt like it was my window – to show my faith, practice what I preach and take the risk. I used to ask myself when I needed the boost, "Hey, what if it does work out?"

The first month was really hard. It was winter and Heath left the house every morning just after 6 a.m. I was alone and felt terribly selfish and guilty. I busied myself with writing and booking new clients, but leaving a corporate career after more than a decade was no easy transition. I had no fellow entrepreneurial friends. Everyone else was at work all day. And what was I doing? I looked at my closet full of blazers and heels and, it sounds silly, but I felt like I no longer had a use for these things that made me feel important. I felt scared, uncertain and I second-guessed myself a lot. Had I done the right thing? I gave up a big income in a booming industry. I lived in one of the most expensive cities in the world. Having come from such a poor family, part of me could not believe myself. Was I stupid?

I flew to the U.K. to visit my mother and came back sad and scared. Very sad. And very scared. It should have been an exhilarating time but big change is tough. There is no sugar coating it.

That lasted about a month. I did my usual LinkedIn updates and responded to recruiters, telling potential employers that I was not interested in full-time positions (feeling unsure and heavy as I did so). And then I had an idea. I wondered if anyone would consider hiring me as a consultant/advisor/coach to help build their business?

I could package my life coaching skills, sales expertise and general business experience and use it to advise senior management at high growth Silicon Valley startups. (D.C. is full of consultants and I had learned what they do and how they work.)

The first two people I shared this idea with met me for coffee. They both wanted to hire me as an adviser for their businesses. I could not believe my luck! Thanks, Universe.

I'm not telling you these stories to gloat. I'm telling you because I want you to know that there are more incredible opportunities around us than we realise, if we remain proactive, receptive and open.

In times of doubt, guard your thoughts like a bulldog. When doubt creeps in, defer to why it WILL work out. I still have a list in my phone of why things will work out for me in any time of my life. They include people who will always hire me, as a back-up plan, a reminder of the size of my awesome online community, and my supportive husband and friends.

I've been obsessed with self-help books since I was a kid and my mom and I would scour secondhand shops for good books at a good discount. Now I am the author of a self-help book.

So, time strapped? Start anyway. Not sure what your passion is? Start anyway. Self-doubting? Start anyway. I got you. Put all doubt, fear and anxiety aside – just for a second – and ask yourself, "What if it does work out?"

Then buckle up. Take a deep breath. And be prepared for it to come true.

Chapter Sixteen:
Still Stuck For Ideas? Check Out These Resources

ONE of the amazing benefits of working in tech for so many years was that I came across so many different peer-to-peer web based marketplaces that make it so easy for aspiring entrepreneurs and side hustlers to hang out their shingle. From dog sitting, to providing legal advice or guided tours, never before has it been so easy to put your product/service in front of millions of prospective customers.

Many of these platforms allow you to set and promote your business *before* you make your first dollar. And given that many of us have multiple passions, promoting our work on several of these allows us to set up multiple revenue streams for our hustle. There really is no excuse; it has never been easier to get started. These are just some of the hundreds of platforms available and are a great way to get the entrepreneurial juices flowing.

Are you secretly a graphic designer?

There are so many opportunities to offer your services online in the design space from building websites to designing books/magazines, business cards, packaging and signage! In fact, I used 99designs to design this book cover and interior and I found my website developer on Fiverr.

99designs (99designs.com) – this hugely successful crowdsourcing marketplace for graphic designers allows designers to read a prospect's brief then compete for the business by providing preliminary design ideas. The prospect will then narrow down a few designs/designers, fine tune the brief and select a winner, who can make anywhere from a few hundred to a few thousand dollars depending on the project. Other platforms include **DesignCrowd (designcrowd.com)** and **crowdSPRING (crowdspring.com)**.

Fiverr (fiverr.com) – another huge marketplace for creative professionals. With Fiverr, you set an initial price of $5 and work upwards depending on additions made to your offering or upselling. There are many success stories of people making thousands of dollars a month offering an array of services from graphics and design to digital marketing, writing, translation, video, animation, music, audio, advertising and more. I read a fascinating story on Business Insider about a former musician who started doing voice overs for $5 a piece on Fiverr – he then started to experiment with video and was able to create more lucrative packages. Long story short, he has since quit his full-time job, paid off $50,000 in debt and makes up to $23,000/month from what started as a side hustle!

Upwork (upwork.com) – similar to Fiverr, Upwork provides a marketplace for web and mobile developers, designers and creatives, accountants, consultants, virtual assistants, translators and copywriters.

Boost Media (boostmedia.com) – if you are a skilled copywriter, Boost Media may be a great platform for you.

Are you a subject matter expert?

This actually comes as a surprise to many of the clients that I coach, but the chances are you are already an expert in at least one area, whether that be your full-time job, side hustle or simply something that interests you. You can monetize that! There are so many avenues you can take to make money as a consultant. When I first transitioned from side hustling to full-time entrepreneur, I consulted (and still do) for a company by the name of Gerson Lehrman Group (GLG), who would pay me to speak with various corporations about digital media and programmatic advertising. This added a fantastic additional revenue stream.

Gerson Lehrman Group/GLG (glg.it) – An American expert network based in New York that acts as a knowledge brokerage between corporations and business leaders, scientists, academics, former public sector leaders and subject matter specialists.

GuidePoint (guidepoint.com) – much like GLG, they connect subject matter experts from more than 100 industry categories across six sectors: Healthcare, Tech, Financial and Business Services, Consumer Goods and Services, Media and Telecom, Energy, Industrials and Basic Materials and Legal and Regulatory. Similar platforms include **The Expert Institute (theexpertinstitute.com)** and **PopExpert (popexpert.com)**.

Do people love your cooking?

You go, Martha Stewart! You can monetize that! This concept was completely unfamiliar to me until our good friend Chris, who is an amazing host and cook, introduced us to the concept of being paid to host dinners for complete strangers in their house, your house or at an independent venue. Whether you are an actual chef, an aspiring chef or simply love to cook for people, there are a number of platforms that allow you to set your menu, time, location, number of people and price! This could be the perfect first step for you to pursue that restaurant/hospitality dream.

Feastly (eatfeastly.com) – From great home cooks to Michelin starred chefs, I have heard of people earning thousands a month from this site.

EatWith (eatwith.com) – Similar to Feastly, EatWith currently has more than 500 people hosting dinners in 150 cities in 30 countries. To date, it has hosted more than 10,000 dinners. You can become a part of the action.

BonAppetour (bonappetour.com) – A slightly different platform that connects local home chefs with travelers, providing them with a unique experience.

CookUnity (cookunity.us) – Think Blue Apron meets Feastly. Based in New York City, CookUnity will give you use of their kitchen space, the best ingredients, packaging and will help you market and distribute meals to foodies. Share your family recipes, your story and build a following.

Love to paint? Fancy yourself as an artisan?

The Internet is bursting with opportunities for aspiring artists and artisans to promote, sell and even loan their work! You can connect with buyers without having a pretentious gallery owner follow them around and judging their ability to come up with the dinero. I have used some of these sites a number of times to browse for anything from wall art for our apartment to linen curtains. These platforms also provide a much cheaper alternative to setting up a retail location or even a market stall. I once had a market stall in Sydney, it was an abnormally cold summer day and it was raining sporadically. I had already paid the non-refundable fee of $250 to reserve my plot so I said "screw it" and set up shop anyway – I sold $150 worth of product – suffice to say the economics of that day didn't work in my favor. Plus I finished the day drenched.

Etsy (etsy.com) – a hugely popular global marketplace that connects buyers and sellers of unique goods both on and offline. The marketplace, with its 24 million active buyers, is a behemoth for creators of anything from clothing to accessories, jewelry, art, crafts and home goods. Etsy takes a transaction fee of 3.5 percent but the platform provides tools and support that make it super easy to promote your product. Similar to Etsy, **Zibbet (zibbet.com)** is also worth looking at.

Artsicle (artsicle.com) – Founded in 2010, Artsicle is one of the hottest platforms that connects artists and sculptors to prospective buyers and has been referred to as the "Zappos for art." It even allows for purchasers to rent the art before making the plunge into either renewing the lease or purchasing the piece. A unique take on the "try before you buy" ideology.

Redbubble (redbubble.com) – An artistic marketplace that connects buyers and sellers of anything from art prints to calendars, canvas prints, phone cases, T-shirts and hoodies, greeting cards and more.

TurningArt (turningart.com) – A fantastic platform that allows artists to rent their work to businesses and homes. Leases can be renewed or the work can even be purchased if still available.

Are you a natural caregiver?

If you are a natural caregiver, whether it be babysitting, caring for the elderly or pet sitting, there are a few great options.

Care.com – this is essentially a one-stop shop for caregivers to provide their services. From babysitters to caring for children with special needs, the elderly, dogs (walking, sitters, grooming, training) to house sitters; Care.com has done a great job of providing a marketplace with 19 million members in 16 countries.

DogVacay (dogvacay.com) – Available across the USA and Canada, DogVacay connects pet owners with more than 25,000 caring sitters. The platform takes care of the administrative side, handling insurance, payment and customer support so that you can just focus on taking care of the animal(s).

Rover (rover.com) is another similar service. In fact, I read a New York Post article stating that, on Rover's platform, full-time sitters average $3,300/month, part-time sitters average $900/month and those with a couple of stays a month average $250. This could be a perfect side hustle for retirees, freelancers, stay-at-home parents or even teachers on summer break.

TalkSpace (talkspace.com) – TalkSpace has helped therapy adapt to the digital age and allows licensed therapists to speak with clients via smartphone or the web.

Know your city well? Speak another language?

Great side hustle opportunities there! My sisters all live abroad. One in Munich, one in Rome, one in Sabah (Malaysia) and one in Surrey, England. The sister in Munich speaks five languages and the one in Rome has lived there for many years and speaks beautifully fluent Italian. While they seldom allow me to lecture them about their side hustlin' potential, they do appreciate that there is a market for their skills. If you are passionate about your city, or linguistic skills, one of these may be for you!

GetYourGuide (getyourguide.com) – You can become a tour guide in your city/region and get paid to do it!

Vayable (vayable.com) – The website sums it up in one sentence, "Discover and book unique experiences offered by local insiders." Anything from offering a food crawl in Rome, to a night time photography tour in Paris, to scouting for street art in San Francisco, to showing people around the hottest spots in New York City's East Village; these are just some examples of what people have offered on their site. You list an experience and if approved, you get the opportunity to make money. Heck, list several if it brings joy!

Verbling (verbling.com) – According to their site, there are 800,000 language learners and 37 languages being taught! Looking briefly at the site, teachers appear to be earning anywhere from $10-$40 an hour based on the pricing they set. The great thing about Verbling is that you can display your schedule and availability online, to avoid any back and forth.

Verbalplanet (verbalplanet.com) – Like verbling, Verbalplanet is a peer-to-peer language site that allows you to set your schedule and rates and earn reviews. Looking at the site, $15-$25 appears to be a reasonable price point for a 45-minute lesson and some of the instructors on the platform have given thousands of lessons.

Feeling geeky or teachy?

Whether you are a full stack engineer, talented coder, great with tech support or simply like to teach or tutor people on an array of subjects, there is a marketplace for your skills.

Geekatoo (geekatoo.com) – If you are the sort of person that has a knack for computer installation/repair, network set up, video game tech support, TV and audio support or smart phone/tablet tech support then Geekatoo may be a great way to earn some extra cash on the side. **HelloTech (hellotech.com)** is a similar marketplace.

HourlyNerd (hourlynerd.com) – This is an impressive service that pairs MBA students and grads, who could not typically afford a big name consulting firm, with business owners to assist with research and projects. HourlyNerd take a 14.5 percent cut but some of the stories I have read have been really impressive, including one woman who left her job and after doing several projects through HourlyNerd landed a three week gig with a multinational company that paid $55,000 to have her help them analyze and redesign their financial process.

CodeMentor (codementor.io) – CodeMentor allows you to put your coding skills to use by pairing you up with those that need some 1:1 help. As a mentor, you would typically charge at least $10 for a 15-minute consultation on the platform and there are people charging much higher.

StudyPool (studypool.com) – This platform allows students to instant message a tutor 24/7 and has helped more than 1 million students. Tutors can set their schedule as to when they are available to help answer homework questions and top earners have exceeded $70,000 in earnings.

WyzAnt (wyzant.com) – Much like StudyPool, this online and in person tutoring platform matches students and tutors across a broad spectrum of subjects and grade levels. Doing a quick search in my postcode for calculus (yuck!) tutors, I saw a range in pricing, from college students and recent grad charging $50/hour to lecturers/faculty/professors charging $200/hour, with many of them having received hundreds of ratings.

Prefer to work in person?

Let's face it, not all hustles can be done with a web cam and a Skype account but there are still plenty of fantastic peer-to-peer marketplaces that match buyers and sellers of services that are delivered/performed in person.

TaskRabbit (taskrabbit.com) – A huge marketplace where you can promote your hustle in anything from handyman services to shopping and delivery, cleaning, moving help or administrative services. "Taskers" can set their own prices and schedules. Looking at the site, there are people charging $10 to as much as $150/hour. Australia has a similar site in **Airtasker (airtasker.com)** as does the U.K. in **Bark (bark.com)**.

Thumbtack (thumbtack.com) – Not entirely dissimilar to TaskRabbit, Thumbtack allows you to offer a broader spectrum of services from photography to singing lessons, tutoring, locksmithing and cooking. The business model is slightly different in that buyers submit a brief/request and service providers pay a nominal fee to bid for the job. The bidding process isn't too overcrowded though with a limit on the number of bidders per job.

Are you a natural coach?

If your calling is to life coaching like mine you will understand that getting exposure and attracting new clients can be pretty tough when starting out. Fortunately there are a couple of platforms dedicated to those looking to coach and teach.

Noomii (noomii.com) – According to the site, they are the web's largest directory of life coaches and business coaches. Potential clients describe their goals and are matched with a coach based on suitability. After the coach and the client have a free 15 minute consult, they can decide whether they want to continue.

Coach.me (coach.me) – Also a life and business coaching database. Members pay an annual fee but this is refunded if you don't earn that back from business garnered through the site.

Udemy (udemy.com) – A huge online education marketplace that allows you to teach online courses from anywhere in the world. It currently has 20,000 instructors, 11 million students, is located in 190 countries and has average instructor earnings of $8,000. Courses on offer cover a wide variety of options from music to design, marketing, personal development, health and fitness, language, test prep, IT and software, and more. Udemy also provides useful tools to help you create your course in a format that is a fit for their platform.

CoachUp (coachup.com) – Are you a former sporting star, looking to give back to the game that brought you so much joy? This may be a great place for you to offer your services. CoachUp allows you to offer private coaching and team sports training in more than 30 sports. You get to decide on your rate and schedule. My husband loves basketball; a quick look at basketball coaches in our area shows me they are charging anywhere from $50-$130 per session.

Wello (wello.com) – Are you a certified personal trainer? This could be the perfect opportunity for you to join the web-based fitness instruction craze, rather than harassing people for 1:1 training at the gym. The platform allows you to set your own hours, provide 1:1 or group coaching and get paid via direct deposit. The beauty here is that, given the digital nature of it, you can teach a global client base in multiple time zones. This is perfect for hustling before and after your day job!

Are you a trusty assistant?

I used to be a recruitment consultant that worked with C-Level executives to hire world class executive assistants, and I can tell you, being a reliable assistant is a true skill. It could also make for a great side hustle and there are quite a few platforms that allow you to let busy people know that you are happy to run errands for them, for a price!

Alfred (helloalfred.com) – You can earn up to $25 an hour for running errands as simple as picking up/delivering laundry, grocery shopping/fridge restocking, house cleaning, tailoring or shoe repair, sorting mail, picking up prescription medication, delivering packages and more.

WeGoLook (wegolook.com) – I found this one to be very interesting. You can earn $25-$200/hour according to their site to perform tasks such as auto inspections, inspection of auction items, property inspections and more. Get paid to check them out, send photos and report back with the details. A friend of ours was looking to buy an investment property down in Charlotte while living in Chicago. Flying back and forth to look at properties would obviously be expensive, so a solution like this (without the bias of a real estate broker) may be a great solution.

My List Of Resources:

While I have certainly used several of these, I have not used them all, but have heard a number of success stories with most. My suggestion would be to research each (as well as others) to see what would be the best fit for your business and financial goals/situation. This should act as a nice starting point though and after reading the preceding chapters, you should be familiar with a few of these.

Website/Blogging Design Platforms

- **WordPress** – My current website was built by my designer using WordPress. It is a very user friendly platform and relatively intuitive, so after the initial set up you should be able to make any minor changes on your own (with perhaps a little help from Google). Many of the most popular blogs were built using WordPress.
- **SquareSpace**
- Disqus – This is a fantastic commenting tool/plug-in that I have seen on many of the more popular blogs and comment-enabled sites. I used it on mine.

Domain Registrars:

- **GoDaddy**
- **Hostgator**

One thing to note is that when you buy your domain, you want to find out whether or not the domain is being hosted on a shared server. This is critical for when traffic to your site increases. As traffic to my site grew, I had issues with my site taking a long time to load due to the fact that it was being hosted on a shared server. I then had it moved to a virtual private server (VPS).

Email/CRM Tools:

- **MailChimp** – I used MailChimp when I first started and really liked it because it was free up to a certain level of subscribers.

- **Ontraport** – Once my business started to scale, I switched to Ontraport as I found it to be a better all-in-one platform for email and product launch management. It isn't cheap though and costs me around $300/month.

- **Infusionsoft** – I was initially leaning toward Infuisionsoft when I switched from MailChimp but decided to go with Ontraport as I felt it was a better fit for my business. Do your homework though. A lot of really successful people use Infusionsoft and find it to be a better fit for them.

- **ConvertKit** – another CRM platform worth checking out.

Payment Processors:

- Paypal
- Square

- Venmo

Virtual Assistant Services:
- Fiverr
- Brickwork India
- YourManInIndia

Creative Services:
- 99designs – they helped me design this very book cover!
- Fiverr

Online Webinar/Teleseminar Services:
- FreeConferenceCall.com
- Citrix GoToWebinar
- WebinarJam

Legal:

I would strongly suggest consulting with a lawyer before setting up shop. Many will do a free consultation, from which you can get a lot of valuable information in terms of the type of legal structure you should set up and ongoing requirements. For a cheaper alternative (and one that I used to set my business up) you may want to look at a company like LegalZoom to help with the legal side at a relatively affordable price.

Accounting:

Choose an accountant that really knows what your business is about. A good accountant will help you maximize the profitability of your business while adhering to any taxation and reporting requirements. I went though a number of accountants before finding one I felt comfortable with. In the last year or so I also hired a bookkeeper. She can do in 1 hour what would take me much longer, so I was happy to pay $70/hour so I could focus on growing revenue. She also has a close working relationship with my accountant, which is ideal.

Be Careful Investing In The Following:

- **Flashy Marketing Materials** – I see so many people blow money trying to make their business and brand as "beautiful as possible" only to make no money. Promotion does not necessarily mean spending loads of cash of shiny things for your business. You can have a clean, engaging brand with relatively minimal cost. I am a huge advocate of making money before spending money.

- **Public Relations** – there are so many hack "PR Expert" types out there that will take your money and yield you very little. If you do insist on hiring someone though, choose someone with great testimonials that fits within your budget. In my experience, the best PR you can do comes from the relationships you build and the value you offer. Relationship building and reciprocity (helping others too – ideally first) is the key!

- **Expensive Advertising (on or offline)** – Be very careful when it comes to spending money on advertising. More often than not, people throw good money after bad. Don't be trapped into thinking that paying for Facebook likes will lead to loads of business. You want to spend wisely so that any advertising is leading to actual conversions (i.e. somebody going to your site and signing up to your subscriber list). I know or know of plenty of people who have big social media followings (much of which was paid for) with tiny email subscriber lists whose businesses make hardly any money. Again, good money after bad.

- **Course After Course After Course** – courses are great, I love paying for a good course if it helps me take my business to the next level and I teach a number of courses. But unfortunately, there are many people that are serial course takers, who wait for that spark of inspiration or the "right time" to launch their business and never take any action. Think back to the Stephen King quote – **Don't be an amateur!**

My Favorite Mindset Resources:

Books

- "Choose Yourself" – James Altucher
- "The Life Changing Magic of Tidying Up" – Marie Kondo
- "The Magic of Thinking Big" – David Schwartz
- "The Little Red Book of Selling" – Jeffrey Gitomer
- "Feel The Fear And Do It Anyway" – Susan Jeffers
- "The Success Principles" – Jack Canfield
- "Life Loves You" – Louise Hay
- "Steal Like An Artist" – Austin Kleon
- "Do The Work" – Steven Pressfield
- "The Law of Divine Compensation" – Marianne Williamson
- "The 4 Hour Work Week" – Tim Ferriss
- "The Art of Non Conformity" - Chris Guillebeau
- "Get Rich Lucky Bitch" – Denise Duffield-Thomas

Plus: Biographies of anyone who inspires you.

Podcasts

- James Altucher
- Tara Brach
- Brendon Burchard
- Rob Bell

- Being Boss
- Michael Hyatt
- Elizabeth Gilbert
- Wayne Dyer
- Tim Ferriss

Hear It From A Hustler: Interviews With People Like You Who Have Started A Side Hustle And Succeeded

Lauren Grant: C.E.O, The Grant Access, New York

The Grant Access, LLC is a full event planning and execution company. They do everything from full services to vendor and sponsor management.

Q: What is your side hustle and how did you decide it was the right one for you?

A: I'd been doing event production for various close friends and non-profits for about 10 years or so. After getting laid off I realized... I can't do this for free anymore. Strangely enough, my epiphany came during a party I was throwing for a friend. It was like the heavens opened up and said, "You are really good at this!" My network heavily influenced my decision to make The Grant Access official. Having their support, encouragement and affirmation of my skills gave me the additional push I needed. I had clients before I even had a business name.

Q. How long have you been doing it?

A. About 12 years now.

Q. How many hours a week (on average) do you dedicate to your side hustle?

A. I like to say, "I have a 9 to 5 and a 5 to 9!" My side hustle takes up about 20-30 hours per week.

Q. What is the longer-term goal of your side hustle?

A. Ideally, as much as I love working in advertising, I'd like to be able to focus solely on my business. Possibly consulting part time and using the rest of the days in my week to grow The Grant Access.

Q. Does your boss know and/or mind?

A. My immediate boss knows but I'm not sure if she knows how much a part of my life this is. I don't think she minds as long as it doesn't interfere in my work.

Q. What keeps you going in moments of stress/fatigue and setbacks?

A. The people that believe in me help a lot and the fact that I know my purpose and passion ensure that life is celebrated in the best way. I like to say, "Life is too short not to have fun." Whether that be a party or a corporate meeting, events should be enjoyable occasions for the host and attendees.

Q. How much revenue (on average) does your side hustle generate per month?

A. Between $1,000-$3,000

Q. What does your side hustle cost (on average) per month?

A. Thankfully I have very little overhead (especially since I can write off things like internet service and my cell phone bill). I'd say on average my costs are around $200.

Q. The hardest thing about side hustlin' is...

A. Finding the energy! It's literally a second full-time job at times, so juggling my side hustle and my full-time work can be challenging. Some nights I'm just not up to another 2-3 hours of work, but I push through it because I KNOW I'm walking in my purpose.

Q. The best thing about side hustlin' is...

A. Working for something that doesn't feel like work. After events I'm usually EXHAUSTED, but I wouldn't trade it for the world. Seeing the smiles on my clients' faces and satisfied guests makes it ALL worth it!

Q. What is your advice for people wanting to get started with a side hustle?

A. Figure out what you're great at and what doesn't feel like work. From there, think about how you can monetize it and start finding ways for you to barter your skills for someone else's (web design, logo, etc.)

Q. Any other tips/advice?

A. CHARGE WHAT YOU'RE WORTH! Even though it's technically a side hustle, it's still a legitimate business. If you do good work, you deserve to be compensated for it. I changed my pricing three times my first year in business. I realized I HATED asking for what I was worth... until I got a client who I didn't charge enough for the work she hired me to do. It changed my outlook on it forever.

Amber Genuske, managing editor of video at a college-based content startup.

While hustling for her main gig, Amber also loves to hustle up freelance projects as a video and multimedia storyteller. Amber is also my rock star photographer and videographer!

Q. What is your side hustle and how did you decide it was the right one for you?
A. Primarily video production with a few photo projects peppered in here or there. I decided it was the right side hustle for me because it was something I was already super passionate about and had the right skillset for.

Q. How long have you been doing it and why did you start it?
A. About four years. I decided to start doing it to make some extra cash. My boyfriend just recently joined my side hustle and I now act as the manager for our duo.

Q. How many hours a week (on average) do you dedicate to your side hustle?
A. These days it's little to none due to a new, super demanding job. A majority of my side hustle is now spent managing my previously mentioned boyfriend who tackles most of the creative work.

Q. What is the longer-term goal of your side hustle?
A: I would love to potentially turn my side hustle into a full-time gig.

Q. Does your boss know and/or mind?
A. Yes and they do not mind. As long as my side hustle isn't a conflict of interest, then I'm good to go. I am also managing a small team of people who each have their own side hustles and I don't mind either. It's pretty inherent to the media world that everyone has a side hustle.

Q. What keeps you going in moments of stress/fatigue and setbacks?
A. I try to not burn out – simple as that. I take frequent breaks and will step back from projects if I think they are weighing on me too much.

Q. How much revenue (on average) does your side hustle generate per month?
A. It varies drastically. Some months it's $300 for one photo shoot, other months I am swimming in projects and can make up to $4,000.

Q. What does your side hustle cost (on average) per month?
A. I have it worked out so that it costs me very little. Maybe a lunch or a coffee every month.

Q. The hardest thing about side hustlin' is...
A. Managing my time ...

Q. The best thing about side hustling' is...
A. Making extra $$$!

Q. What is your advice for people wanting to get started with a side hustle?

A. Never be afraid of the hustle. I think too many people think they can't make it happen for a number of (usually valid but ultimately able-to-overcome) excuses. It may seem daunting, but just get that first project under your belt and you will learn, iterate, and improve as you go.

Q. Any other tips/advice?

A. Be smart with your time, don't get overwhelmed with too much work so that you can't meet expectations, and never work for free.

Aaron Clausen, C.E.O, Nature Mapr.

NatureMapr helps organizations collect, manage and analyze information from the natural world.

Q. What is your side hustle and how did you decide it was the right one for you?

A. NatureMapr happened by accident when I almost trampled over the most critically endangered rare plant colony in the Australian Capital Territory – the Canberra Spider Orchid. I later learned that I had been ignorantly mountain biking on an illegally formed track that I wasn't meant to be riding on. It moved me and made me realize how delicate and sensitive these plants were. I almost wiped out half the last remaining colony on earth! I partnered with government to form the Canberra Nature Map project (http://CanberraNatureMap.org) and the project's success really blew me away. We rounded up all the ACT's rare plant (and soon to be animal) experts and basically formed a working partnership with the government.

Q. How long have you been doing it?

A. NatureMapr was founded in January 2016, but my involvement with Canberra Nature Map kicked off in September 2013.

Q. How many hours a week (on average) do you dedicate to your side hustle?

A. 40-60 hours per week. It is more than a full-time job, in addition to my full-time job!

Q. What is the longer-term goal of your side hustle?

A. It has never been to be "rich and famous." It has always simply been to be able to do what I absolutely love on a full-time basis.

Q. Does your boss know and/or mind?

A. My employers (the federal government) are aware of my extra-curricular activities and actually think it's pretty cool. The first thing is that within government you have to declare external activities and potential conflicts of interest on an annual basis. So NatureMapr is legitimately declared. But it actually gets you a bit of "street cred" in the technology workplace as well because it's a technology company that you've built by hand and, well, I work in technology. So you're living what you preach rather than just talking about doing something one day.

Q. What keeps you going in moments of stress/fatigue and setbacks?

A. To me, it's like this big job with a huge end goal that I just need to complete and take it to the point where anyone in the world can use it and get the benefits. The other thing that inspires me are all the outcomes from the work which are extremely important. So when I see that someone reported a sighting of a single koala within an area that was about to be demolished or wiped out and because of the software platform that I built by hand, that development application got rejected, you can't imagine the buzz I get from that – it actually gives me shivers. It certainly beats developing a boring government intranet system!

Q. How much revenue (on average) does your side hustle generate per month?

A. $10,000

Q. What does your side hustle cost (on average) per month?

A. Lots. Particularly in the early days. While I do all the web/database/server/API coding work myself directly, which is obviously a massive cost saver, I've made significant investment in our mobile application platform by bringing in an expert mobile developer. As a result our mobile platform is absolutely first class and the best in the world to my knowledge. But the reason I've been able to make that investment is because I have strong cash flow coming in from my federal government contract – otherwise there is no way I'd be able to take that risk.

Q. The hardest thing about side hustlin' is...

A. When your day job stress is at its peak, for example just before a major release that you've been working on for 12 months, and then at the same time your side hustle wins two more customer projects and you have no choice but to stay up until midnight all week to deliver those projects. Somehow I've become pretty desensitized to stress and good at just plugging on regardless.

Q. The best thing about side hustlin' is...

A. You have reduced your level of risk, you don't need to dilute your company and take external investment and you can do it on your own terms. You are your own boss.

Q. What is your advice for people wanting to get started with a side hustle?

A. Cash flow is critically important. Whatever you do, you have to maintain regular cash flow throughout the entire period by doing whatever you can. So don't run off all inspired with the dream to build the next famous app and quit your day job. I learnt this lesson by starting another business many years ago where I walked away from regular cash flow to put it all on the line. Even if you make insane progress with the business, you soon find that cash flows through businesses much more erratically than it does through a regular day job. But by having regular cash flow (even if it means working another day job for a while that you aren't in love with), it means you can keep going.

Q. Any other tips/advice?

A. Another lesson I learnt the hard way in the past was trying to build or design a business based on where I thought there was an obvious gap and/or opportunity in the market. But what I found was that nobody cared about what I was doing. It was so hard to get any help or interest in what I was doing. News flash: I was in fact doing it for the wrong reasons. I had started that business to "try to be successful". It was four years of huge slog, the hardest I've ever worked in my life, and I was only lucky to be able to get out by offloading it to a much larger fish in the pond. I wouldn't recommend that approach. The funny thing about NatureMapr is that when I hit rock bottom after much business and career stress I just started going mountain biking, bush walking and wandering outdoors to escape all my stresses as a way to kind of meditate and chill out. And it was exactly there, where I loved what I was doing, that my next business found me. I definitely didn't force it and it just happened on its own. Don't force it, do what you love.

Dan Kolansky – C.E.O, Champions Of The Web

Q. What is your side hustle and how did you decide it was the right one for you?

A. I build websites and Internet marketing campaigns for companies. I used to run an I.T. company and so many people started asking me for marketing and development help that I eventually decided it was worth making the shift.

Q. How long have you been doing it and why did you start it?

A. I've been building websites for 17 years. I've built them professionally for 14 years, and I have run my own business around building websites and marketing since 2007. I started my own business when I got married in 2006. It was my primary source of income while I finished school. I eventually picked up a full-time job to help provide stability in my life and bring in extra income, but kept the business rolling.

Q. How many hours a week (on average) do you dedicate to your side hustle?

A. About 30 hours a week.

Q. What is the longer-term goal?

A. Right now, to raise my income. It allows my wife to stay home with the kids and funds my love of hobbies like photography and camping. Long term, I want to build up to personal financial freedom and get the chance to spend the majority of my time with my family and on community-building in my area. Ironically, my business has gifted financial freedom to several of my clients already. Time to do it for myself.

Q. Does your boss know and/or mind?

A. My boss knows of it and has even referred me business over the years. I try not to rub his nose in it, though. When clients ask where I'm spending my time, I often refer to my job as another client. All in all I try to keep the two worlds from crossing paths as much as I can. It doesn't always work as planned, but so far they live in relative harmony.

Q. What keeps you going in moments of stress/fatigue and setbacks?

A. I watch a LOT of TV! Sadly, recharging is a consistent need of mine and I spend more time than I should on Reddit, YouTube, and watching television. It helps fill the cracks in my day and gives me a chance to unwind before the next big push. When things go really wrong, I often will just call the day a wash and make sure I get a shower and a solid night's sleep. Sleep is a common culprit for me making mistakes. So getting a good night's sleep often fixes any attitude issues I have and gives me a fresh view when I come back the next morning.

Q. How much revenue (on average) does your side hustle generate per month?

A. Right now it hovers around $60-70K/year. But I'm aiming to double or triple that in the next 12 months.

Q. What does your side hustle cost (on average) per month?

A. I spend about $1,000/month on various technical expenses.

Q. The hardest thing about side hustlin' is...

A. Finding time to get everything done! You find yourself answering emails in the bathroom, taking showers at 3 in the morning (one day that is the end of your day, and another day it is when you got up so you can finish a project before presentation time), and forgetting to eat balanced meals (if you eat at all).

Q. The best thing about side hustlin' is...

A. Your income isn't capped and neither are your horizons. If you don't like your job for some reason you can just tell them to pound sand and move on with your life. It also makes you more valuable to your job. If they know that your side gig is giving you equal or more income then the power in the relationship moves to you. They need you and you don't need them. This makes it very easy to ask for special treatment, extra vacation, raises, or the like. I haven't taken advantage of this positioning as much as I probably should have, but it has given me confidence in communicating with my boss (which actually improved our relationship).

Q. What is your advice for people wanting to get started with a side hustle?

A. You can't be everything to everyone. You need to 1, stop caring what other people think of you working a second "job." You are officially going to be misunderstood for a long time. People won't understand or appreciate why you're working at home at 6pm instead of goofing off with them. And 2, you need to become obsessive about systems and automation. Build your business to run itself, write form responses to all your common email and phone interactions. If your business offers a service or product, you should have an instruction guide written on how to do every single step.

Q. Any other tips/advice?

A. Automate, automate, automate. Ubot Studio is fantastic software which I use to make automation scripts for myself and my clients. It has made me 1000 times more productive and enabled me to be hyper responsive to my day job and my business. Get it, master it, and implement it in your business.

Become a business and marketing junkie. I collect business training like people collect spoons or stamps. I have books, podcasts, video courses, and more. Other people have incredible ideas and it is good to collect those ideas, mix and match in your own projects and improve your overall life. The info products I purchase for my business also positively impact my day job. I actually have them pay me a small amount to my business, which allows me to list them as a "client", and so I can use all kinds of tools and software to make my day job better. This makes me look like a rock star at work and gives me more time to work on my own projects.

Also, work from home if you can. Get out from under the prying eyes of your boss. They just want to see results and if you can give that, there is no reason you should be sitting around browsing Facebook in the extra spaces of your day. A client call here, or quick knocking out a project there gets a lot easier when you're working from home. If you want to find a path to work from home then Tim Ferriss' "The 4-Hour Workweek" gives a pretty good way to get there. I also consult with people on occasion on how to make it happen as well.

Ady Wright, C.E.O – the Verbal Gold Blog, Atlanta

Q. What is your side hustle and how did you decide it was the right one for you?

A. Verbal Gold Blog was actually started for me by a friend and called When In Doubt Just Add Glitter. After a year and some time off I decided to take blogging seriously, rebranded to Verbal Gold and decided to make this passion of mine for profit.

Q. How long have you been doing it and why did you start it?

A. Verbal Gold Blog was started in January of 2015

Q. How many hours a week (on average) do you dedicate to your side hustle?

A. I don't allocate a certain amount of hours to my blog's success. I just don't stop or sleep until it's done. Sometimes I go to bed at 6am and other times at 1am. Weekends are usually booked with blog obligations and setting time aside to write plus planning for the week/month ahead.

Q. What is the longer-term goal?

A. Long term I'd love to transition to full-time blogging – specifically in travel. I plan to write a book and I also have a few other things up my sleeve.

Q. Does your boss know and/or mind?

A. My boss, my coworkers, and all of my clients know I have a blog. Most of my clients have actually recommended my blog and me to their friends and introduced me to their brand contacts to work with which is ultimately the biggest compliment. That's how Verbal Gold ended up in this book! Luckily I'm able to do both while still respecting my career and company thanks to apps like Latergramme, Hootsuite, and Buffer, which allow you to schedule postings across all social media sites. It's easy for me to set up weeks out and still focus on my job during the day.

Q. What keeps you going in moments of stress/fatigue and setbacks?

A. The vision. And typically it's just a little overwhelming since there are not enough hours in the day. There is never enough time. But I'm so passionate there is really no stress or fatigue to complain about. It's all worth it when you're the boss. Like they say, put on some gangster rap and handle it. I recommend making a batch playlist for a little extra motivation. You can always steal mine from my blog. (wink)

Q. What else do we need to know?

A. I currently make over six figures (in my day job) and although money is important and the angle/end game for some, the bigger picture is being your own boss, being an entrepreneur and creating something for yourself. That dream is always what keeps me going. The Verbal Gold Blog has expanded to three countries and over seven states in the U.S. in less than a year. Having a good group of girlfriends and like-minded individuals around you only brings you up. I believe in sending the elevator back down and helping those around you.

Sarah Kurtenbach, co-owner of Legacy Investment Team, LLP

Legacy Investment Team, LLP invests in flipping homes and purchasing rental properties.

Q. What is your side hustle and how did you decide it was the right one for you?

A. My side hustle is being a co-owner of an investment company called "Legacy Investment Team, LLP". I have always been intrigued with the real estate market, but did not want to pursue it full time. I also liked the idea of being an investor vs. a manager, contractor or real estate agent. It allows me to make great income back without having to put much time in.

Q. How long have you been doing it and why did you start it?

A. I first invested in flipping a home in Northern California in 2013. A man I trusted told me he was flipping houses on the side, but his money was currently tied up in his other properties. He asked me if I would be willing to be an investor, allowing me to make a percentage back after the house sold. It typically takes 6-8 months to see a return, but the time you put in is just at the beginning and the end for all of the legal documents. After my first successful house flip, I invested to flip homes in 2014 and 2015. Now, I'm using that money to buy rental properties to hopefully build a property portfolio.

Q. How many hours a week (on average) do you dedicate to your side hustle?

A. At the beginning, I have to put in about 3-5 hours to work with the lawyer and the head contractor. This is to ensure everyone is on the same page on the amount that will be invested, the percentage that will be gained after the property sells, and that if anything bad were to happen the money I invested would be protected and returned. After that I'm pretty hands off.

Q. What is the longer-term goal?

A. The main goal is to build a portfolio of rental properties to start making substantial monthly income. I've also brought my dad and brother into the investment business, so we can purchase bigger and larger properties and build a legacy for the generations to come in our family. Our BIG goal is to be able to use a percentage of our profits to do really amazing things around our country and the world. We would like to build schools, doctor clinics and churches, as well as go on mission trips and sponsor mission trips for others.

Q. Does your boss know and/or mind?

A. When I first started investing on the side, my boss did not know. Now, I am my own boss as I also started my own social media and business growth consulting company. I love being able to have multiple streams of revenue and also dabble in different industries.

Q. What keeps you going in moments of stress/fatigue and setback?

A. In the Legacy Investment Team, what keeps me going is that we have a greater goal in mind and our goal is bigger than ourselves.

Q. How much revenue (on average) does your side hustle generate per month?

A. Currently, for every house the Legacy Investment Team flips, we make anywhere from $20,000-$30,000 in profit (depending on how much we invest and the terms).

Q. What does your side hustle cost (on average) per month?

A. The cost is very minimal, as the only costs we have are the legal fees. This is typically a couple hundred dollars per house.

Q. The hardest thing about side hustlin' is...

A. The hardest part about investing in properties as a side business is knowing if the house will be a great return or a total flop. Just like any investment, there is a risk, and you have to be willing to risk everything you put in for a large return. Thankfully, we haven't had any flops yet!

Q. The best thing about side hustlin' is...

A. Being able to continually grow more and more after every investment. Currently, we have not taken any money out of the investment company. We use it all to purchase bigger and better properties. Plus, as the investment company grows, it means we can DO more good!

Q. What is your advice for people wanting to get started with a side hustle?

A. Try it! There is no harm in starting something on the side. I have a lot of friends who offer their talent as a service, e.g. graphic design, website development. They are saving money by not having to purchase products. I have some friends who are able to pay their rent/mortgage with their side hustle!

Q. Any other tips/advice for wannabe hustlers?

A. Usually, a side hustle is based on a passion you have. What is your passion? If it's being creative, maybe you could start a part-time interior design business. If it's working with money, maybe you could help others in their finances? If it's writing, maybe you could start a blog? Make sure it's fun and that you enjoy it!

Anna Goldstein, founder of Self In The City life coaching

Q. What inspired you to take this route?

A. In my twenties, I was trying to figure out my life. Navigating a lot of transitions with relationships, jobs, trying to figure out how to balance my finances and really become the person I wanted to become – a successful adult. I heard many of my friends having the same struggles and I decided to start a website that would offer life tips. Originally I interviewed experts in different areas and wrote a newsletter. In some respects I started it because I needed help and knew I wasn't alone. There's a saying "when you help others, you help yourself."

Q. A lot of people's biggest block to starting a business is the fear of rejection and/or failure. How did you overcome this?

A. I was more afraid of not having something to fall back on. I was afraid of being subject to someone else telling me my destiny – when I could take time off of work, how much I got paid, what creative projects I could do. I wanted to be in charge of my destiny. If I got fired from a job, I wanted something else. I focused on what I loved to do and put my energy into having fun with creation. I didn't think much about failing because I saw working for someone else as the worst possible scenario.

Q. What keeps you going in moments of exhaustion/fatigue and stress?

A. Honestly I didn't set my business up to make me exhausted, stressed or fatigued. If it is going to make me those things, I choose not to do it (that's why I'm the boss). There are moments where I doubt myself, my abilities, and am not sure how I am going to overcome challenges. My passion and purpose helps me. What keeps me going is helping others and feeling connected to my purpose. I let it pull me and I don't push. As Rumi said, "Let yourself be silently drawn to what you love." My business is an extension of my heart and soul. I let that energy pull me to create. I also make sure I walk away and come back to things. In moments of doubt, I get support. I'm a coach and I'm a big believer in having coaches to support you. I talk to other entrepreneurs and surround myself with people who can understand my struggles and offer guidance.

Q. What is your #1 piece of entrepreneurial advice for a beginner (including a side hustler)?

A. Start. Don't wait to be perfect or have it all together. When I first started my coaching business my life was a mess. As I helped others, my life improved. Market yourself before your ready. Don't quit your job – keep your job or find a bridge job until you're making enough money to eliminate your job. Take actions that will make you money directly. It can be easy to get distracted by all the pretty things but focus on closing deals and getting clients. It will boost your confidence by doing it.

Q. What would you say is the best thing about entrepreneurial life so far?

A. Being able to design my own schedule and dictate how much money I make. I'm able to work twice a week and make a full-time income while being home with my son. I have so much flexibility it's priceless.

Q. What has been the biggest surprise about entrepreneurial life?

A. How much personal development matters. As an entrepreneur you are your business. If you have blocks in your mind, you will have blocks in your business. It's a journey of self-improvement and it's so important to never stop learning or investing in yourself.

Q. What is the best business advice you have been given?

A. I got this advice when I first started. "You don't have to get it right, you just have to get it going." Perfectionism will slow you down. It's about progress. Put your best foot forward and put your service out there. Test the market, gain experience. Don't give up but be willing to adjust if you need to.

Q. If you could go back and tell yourself at the very start of launching your coaching business something, what would it be?

A. Don't be afraid to put yourself out there. Not everyone will like you and that's ok. And you can't help everyone. Focus on your fans and who you can help.

Q. You are a C.E.O. and a mom. What is your #1 productivity hack to have a full life and business?

A. Schedule it! If it doesn't go in my schedule it doesn't get done. Whether it be working on my business or going to a meditation class or date night, it must go on the calendar. I block time for different days and activities. I don't over schedule. I make sure I accomplish one business goal a day.

Q. Many people don't start a business because they feel that a large sum of capital is needed to get things going. What do you feel are the essentials for getting a business up and running on a shoestring budget?
A.

1. The right mindset. Period. There is a tendency for people to think they need more of something in order to start. In my heart, I believed in myself. This is not the truth. When I started my business I did not have a large sum of money or a big salary. I had a vision and a purpose. With these two elements, I was able to find ways that were free.

2. I built my own website and learned about ways I could market myself online that wouldn't cost a dime. It's about being resourceful. I had a crappy website that took me to making 6-figures.

3. I also sought mentors who were ahead of me that I could learn from. I learned from other coaches how they built their business.

4. Network. Build relationships. Be authentic, genuine and of service and people will remember you.

5. Read. If you don't know how to do something, read about it. Google it.

6. Don't give up! Be persistent.

"There comes a special moment in everyone's life, a moment for which that person was born... When he seizes it... It is his finest hour."
~*Winston Churchill*–

Why start a hustle?

You really wanna know why?
It's not for the money. It's not to be a C.E.O. of something.
It's not to have full creative control or to one day hand in
that overdue resignation letter.
It's 'cause you have to.

'cause you are good enough.
'cause you matter.
'cause your contribution matters.

Yes, I can give you tips and tricks and shortcuts that
hopefully save you some frustration, assure you that you are
not alone on this journey and hopefully make your long
nights at your laptop, studio or workshop a little easier. But
what is more important than the structure, the advice, the
wisdom from others gathered here? Your inner wisdom. The
wisdom that's compelling you to create something. That
whisper that pushes you forward, the one won't let up even
when you feel down. The voice that urges you to forge
ahead.

Honor that wisdom. It's not wrong. It asks you, "Hey, what
if it does work out?"

So let's find out.

~ ~~THE END~~ ~ *The Beginning...*

Endnotes

A big thank you to Greatist, Business Insider, Huffington Post, News.com.au and Hearst, who allowed me to use parts of my published articles in this book.

An extra special thanks to Heath Collins, Hannah Tattersall, Locke Hughes, Rysia Trembeth and every single kick ass interviewee in this book for making it all possible.

Made in the USA
Middletown, DE
02 December 2016